THE UPS AND DOWNS OF GROWING OLDER: BEYOND SEVENTY YEARS OF LIVING

THE UPS AND DOWNS OF GROWING OLDER: BEYOND SEVENTY YEARS OF LIVING

Viola B. Mecke, Ph.D., ABPP

To order additional copies of this book, contact:
Xlibris
844-714-8691
www.Xlibris.com
Orders@Xlibris.com
837532

I do what I do

For I am who I am

From Paula Kunst
(Eighty years of age)

CONTENTS

PROLOGUE

To The Complexities Of Aging

This book comes from my heart. It is rooted in encounters with crises brought by growing into the oldest-old phase of life Past experiences of family and friends growing older, some dying, marks the significance of each day and the meaningfulness of life. Aging brings personal and social crises that are often inevitable and seldom anticipated. The loss of health, of energy, of memory, even of thinking, in those dear to me was ever refreshed by their creative re-adjustments to changes compelled by age. I am constantly amazed by the vigor of the oldest-old persons who are determined to make a day satisfying, to retain an empathic concern for others and a reflective interest in the world about them.

Our society is a youth-oriented and youth-admiring culture. The technocratic culture is foreign to most oldsters who stumble with the use of cellphones, with computers, of "clouds". It is the world of youth, with infants-in-a-crib delighted by play with video toys. Even though an increasing percentage of the population falls in the older ages, our society is beset by failures to understand or to respect or to revere the aged – as has been so in past generations. Societal reaction has brought increasing discrimination and anger towards elders, in neglect and abusiveness. The growth of "independent living" housing is subtle isolation of the aged, while presented as ideal communities for them. Consequently, while we accept the idiosyncrasies of adolescents, oldness in the population is rued.

The Complexity of Aging is written to describe the conflicts and clarify the difficulties encountered by the oldest of persons as they meet the problems of whether to leave their home, of alterations in physical propensities, of immense losses of social relationships, and strengthening or impairment of personality characteristics. Over seventy-five percent will experience hearing problems and visual difficulties and have suffered more than two chronic illnesses.

I have tried to include insights into problems and conflicts besetting the oldest-old which hopefully will make their pathway more secure and predictable. Understanding the awful normality of changes will enable some acceptance for adjustment to changes, and lessen the confusion, anxiety, and depressive reaction for the person, the family, and friends. These last days add sorrows that oldest age brings. One friend developed neurological decompensation of his spine. Assisted living has been recommended by medical professionals so that he receive necessary care. A strong, independent person and yes, stubborn, who had roller-skated about the community, now will be living in an institution, mostly a solitary existence. Life brings unpredictable problems and ends. How can life be gratifying and peaceful facing the end?

My perspective has been to bring an understanding of and help for the individual oldest-old person and thereby to reinforce the love-bonding with families and friends.

I thank all those who have contributed to the years of accumulated experiences that now brighten my oldest years. Yes, there have been shades and shadows, but I have learned that the dark spots in life add a colorful richness that cannot be denied.

Memories and gratefulness to those most important in my past begin with my parents who were always encouraging, especially when my pathway was different from their expectations. Six siblings added intimate interactions with their unique approaches to life. My brother Bill, five years younger than I, read each chapter and commented frankly to me on the readability of the writing.

In clinical work, patients enriched my knowledge of attitudes toward, and perspectives of acts and emotions used while adjusting to their life's world. While writing, good friends were patient with my withdrawal from social events and cheered me to continue.

A special, warm heartfelt thanks for the editing and critical reading that Marilyn Fitzpatrick provided for each chapter. She offered professional insights throughout these three years of writing, even though she too confronted the complexities of aging. She also suggested the title., "The complexities of Aging...After 75 years." Another special friend, Murray Laurie, professional par excellence, urged me to finish the book even after she had struggled with and edited an incomplete draft. So here it is, dear Reader. It is my wish that it can clarify some of your complexities while aging.

Chapter One

After Seventy – Growing Older-Old

The waves of life tossed us back and forth as we wended our way through the insecurities of youth. During our middle ages, the waters became more rhythmic, rocking us back and forth as life came in waves of life's events that were gentler, even predictable. As the waves now approach the shore of life, they slow in soft, easy motion. Often the waves gently roll over the sands eventually to become still. Ahh, one says, the ideal is to come to the shore of life with calm and peacefulness. But waves hit a rocky shore and in their weakened energy, bounce a bit before their waters ease. And such is life.

We have been through the period of worrying about the wrinkles on our face that started twenty years (at least) ago. They are now a part of our daily appearance. Although we may still fuss with our hair, we no longer sit for hours to disguise its graying. Men quietly watch the graying of beard and hair, and as each hair falls, carefully comb over the emerging bald spot. Our bodies that have carried us through the years have become weakened and bent; walking is a chore for at least seventy-five percent of us – with or without walkers or canes. Walking is slower, our gait and steps, smaller, our arms seem shorter, our feet a bit longer. Our vision is not quite as sharp, and hearing has lost acuity; These continuing changes bring a bit of emotional pain, a quiet protest to the alterations of our being, and then a rueful smile for life is here.

Permit me to introduce myself. I am, by past profession, a psychologist. I am ninety-two years old, and I live in an independent living community. Three years ago, I sold my home in one state, and then re-established myself in another. About twenty years ago I became widowed following my husband's death. Fortunate to enjoy good health despite a serious bout with cancer, I hope to let the ripples of the waters move me gently toward this final journey of life.

I have always enjoyed writing, although mostly professional reports; and my urge to write remains strong. The topics I know best are the emotional challenges of life as they trouble or soothe the pathway. I am especially concerned with the emotional challenges that come to us through this later time of life – often unexpectedly. Emotional challenges still arouse strong feelings, but I have noted that reactions now seem more in balance with the severity of a situation, are more modified to bring resolution, and more easily accepted simply as "a part of life." It is these challenges, some anticipated and others not expected, that I wish to address in this book.

My concern is about the lives of relatively few people, those older-old persons born before 1950. This book deals with living long, representing those who have enjoyed good health, good medical care, and good nutrition, with some genetic help from forebearers. For those born about 1930, the average length of life was sixty years; in other words, one half of those born in 1930 had died by 1990. By 1950 life expectancy was about 68 years; and for those born in 2010, the average person could expect to live about 78 years. During those years between 1950 and 2010, people could expect to live almost twenty years longer than their parents. For those born about 1920, 37% were still alive at 75 years of age in 2013.; for those aged 85 ten percent were living and those aged 95, less than .8 percent were living.[1]

There are indications that the average years of life may *decrease* in the next years because of the prevalence of chronic illnesses, such as diabetes, overeating and tobacco smoking, that are currently increasing. Yet the indications are that about one-fourth of the population will soon be over 75 years of age and it is for these persons that this book is being written.

Growing older than old is a normal period of human life. It comes when the waves slow down and then stop, with dying. We, the older-old, have enjoyed more time in life than most. Often the term "older-old" is applied to those over seventy-five or eighty years. Time cannot be stopped, nor its speed increased. Sometimes it passes slowly for many a day, or too quickly, as the months or years speed by.

As we have lived thus far, we have successfully passed through several phases of life that mark growth into adulthood. Now, beginning about the age of fifty, we enter periods of growth and decline that characterize the second half of life. The Midlife Re-evaluation Phase, commonly known as the midlife crises, now comes. It is a time marked by physical changes bringing messages that the beauty of youth is fading. Relationships with children take on a new flavor as they enter adulthood; relationships with a spouse may meet a significant change because the couple now is facing the awareness of growing older; and, thoughts turn toward retirement and growing older. When a good partnership has developed, individual preferences, activities and even idiosyncrasies are honored by the partner.

It is a time for questions such as: *Who am I? what have I accomplished? How soon will I retire?*

What do I want from life?

When retirement arrives, a new period of life begins – liberation from the control of others. For many, the years following retirement are marked by freedom from meeting the expectations of a working environment. Release from the stress of employment and daily demands may be exhilarating. For some it is the opportunity to spend more time with the family and time for activities that have been placed on the back burner for a long time. Others have fears and apprehensions, for they have few plans for themselves. And for others, there are feelings of regret or a loss of an identity for themselves.

An urge to see the world arises from curiosity of how others live. Traveling brings new experiences to be enjoyed and explored. Comments as, "if not now, when?" reinforce the sense of freedom form life's expectations and responsibilities. Mark Twain wrote: "The seventieth birthday? It is the time of life when you arrive at a new and awful dignity; when you throw aside the decent reserves which have oppressed you for a generation and stand unafraid and unabashed upon your seven-terraced summit and look down and teach unrebuked." A desire for experimentation and an urge to try new activities need honored.

Example: On lady, Jane, retiring after 25 years of an exhausting and stressful job, felt unusually liberated. She moved from a smog-ridden city to a small town and devoted her time to painting pictures, making jewelry, woodcarving and glass molding. Her talents became financially rewarding. Then, she wanted to see the country. She purchased a motor home and travelled from one coast to the other. Now at 72, she was fulfilling yet another lifetime dream. Ever since her grandfather had placed her on a horse when she was four or five years old, she had wanted a horse. She bought a fourteen-year-old well-trained horse, took riding lessons, and enjoyed riding toward the sunset.

Example: Bruce, aged 74, had been reared in an alcohol-free home. After retirement from his law firm, he first explored soap-making. Then, satisfied with that, he set up his own beer-making in the basement of his house and claimed it atoned for his many years of abstinence!

THE SUMMING UP PERIOD:

Did you ever hear the expression that "all he ever talks about is the olden days?" I listen carefully to the topics of discussion older-old persons. A change in topics has taken place. There were few discussions of world events, instead groups of aging persons would talk about and share childhood events and life experiences that were significant, sometimes comic, to them all. And rightly so. For this period of life, called the Summing Up Period (usually ages 75-85), refers to a need for recapitulation of life's events. The desire to share one's life and its significant events with children and grandchildren provides a continuity to one's life. Writing an autobiography or family history brings memories to the fore, adding significance to the lessons learned or missed. Reviews of one's life and sharing histories with others often brings a different perspective to an old event, enriching the sense of self and self-esteem.

Feelings of well-being persist for many as they grow older. Gaining a perspective on the stresses, high points, even missteps of earlier life leads to a self-acceptance that promotes inner contentment. Yes, there are bitter or guilt-loaded memories that can now be accepted as forgiveness and understanding of one's actions. Self-acceptance expressed as acknowledging that "I did the best I could with what I knew at the time" revokes a guilt-loaded conscience, bringing a balance to one's life. Retrospection about missed pathways develops a philosophical view that yields an understanding of choices made in the past.

An important, positive change in attitude may occur as the person looks for a larger purpose in life. The desire to contribute to others leads to attempts to pass on lessons or stories of one's life to the younger generation, both to provide a picture of the older generation, and also to contribute knowledge about the life that was typical of their time. These are the "keepers of the culture." Singing over the river and through the woods" at Thanksgiving made sense to presently aged persons, although they had probably never experienced a sleigh ride to grandmother's house. Grandchildren find the stories almost magical. These memories enter our cultural lore.

Another facet of the Summing Up phase is the desire to contribute to others, to the community, even to the greater culture. Volunteer work for the community beckons many. Philanthropic contributions provide another outlet for other satisfactions. Social relationships usually shrink during this period, gradually, but surely. Relationships focus increasingly more on family, close friends, and familiar institutions as church. A typical change during this time is a growing detachment from people, things, and former desires. Non-attachment brings an ability to care deeply about others, and to let go of a sense of self-importance as the relativity of life is accepted.

Recalling long-lived bitter conflicts now with a family member or friend now seem unimportant and the conflicts without value. Now, understanding the conflict in a different perspective leads to a ???

The Encore Phase brings self-reflection, desire for continuation, and for celebration of life, present and past. *Encore in* French is defined as "again," and this is a recall to the stage of life. It is a desire for continuation and for celebration. This is the swan song, a desire for generations to continue, even with all the dangers that surround us in this technological world. There is a tremendous sense of celebration on those later birthdays; parties are welcome, cards are special remembrances of past experiences and of special people.

There is every reason to expect the escalator to go downward at a faster pace. Life is approaching an ending. The end is near. Yet, the number of persons living more than 85 years is increasing. Generally, the stereotypes of old age define this stage – dependency, illness, decrepitude or wrinkled, wizened and worn. Unlike previous stages, The Encore Phase is characterized by an excess of women over men, higher levels of multiple ailments and an increased number living in institutions.[2]

There is good news for those of us still living during this time. There is evidence that the proportion of disabled elderly is *decreasing*; The age when a person may suffer multiple functional impairment and ailments is *increasing*. This means that we may remain in relatively good health longer, yet endure more prolonged illnesses.

The thoughts of losing cognitive abilities and of dementia are powerful fears for us in this stage. One study followed persons age 75 and older for thirteen years. They found that 49 percent retained good thinking abilities; fifty-one percent showed decline during these years. All showed notable decline in the two years preceding death.[3]

Generally, the Encore Phase is characterized by a functional breakdown of the psychological system – memory, learning skills, reasoning abilities – all show decline during these years. The escalator is stopping for most.

The sense of well-being and satisfaction with life slowly decreases. Positive feelings decrease as the stress of physical ailments, pain, and distress over losing energy and stamina lessen. Even so, it is a matter of the individual. In one study three groups were identified: One group of individuals who had a desirable outlook on life were characterized by a higher level of cognitive performance, maintained many personal goals, enjoyed interests and hobbies, but were involved in a smaller social network.

A second group had average intellectual abilities, a disposition to relish and appreciate life, and an exceptionally large social network. Their lives focused on the presence with others and engaging in social activities, e.g., playing games as bridge, poker, or scrabble. The third group had fewer desirable traits, a dissatisfaction with life and the environment, irritating psychological dependence on others, anxiety, and tenseness, and less of a sense of wellbeing. These are the grumpy ones, fearful of the present and the future.

Life is approaching an ending. The number of persons living more than 85 years is increasing. There will be more persons to share this time of life. Unlike previous stages, there are higher levels of multiple ailments and disabilities, and an increased number living in institutions.

We shall now turn to the challenges we face in these two periods of life. Yes, they are the same but, oh so different. The physical and psychological changes become an immense preoccupation, and we can identify and suffer the effects on life. We shall discuss problems of finding a secure place to live, of the differences in family interactions as adult children and aged parents both grow older, of the loss of motility, of aloneness with the loss of spouses and friends, of the relationship patterns with new friends, of dealing with autonomy and dependence, and, finally, a few notes on the process of meeting dying and death. It is my hopes these words may help to make these last years more pleasant, comfortable, and understandable for all of us.

Growing old has never been fun.

1. ???
2. ???
3. ???

CHAPTER TWO FINAL

Who Are We? What Has Changed?

"The older we grow, the greater becomes our ordeals. (Goethe}
***Periods of calm soothe. Times of perfect stillness are present
when not a ripple ruffles the water. It is almost eerie for the
quietness portends an oncoming storm. But oh, so peaceful; so
beautiful. A sense of an oncoming storm, of rougher riverbeds
ahead do not despoil the calm. The storm will come as it may.***

Retirement has brought relief from work, lesser
expectations, and greater anticipations. Growing-older-
than old brings a singular perspective on life. As the age
of 75 is left behind, a sense of awe accompanies a realization
of being older, even more than just old. We have lived years
longer than others born at the same time – ninety per cent
of our generation are no longer living.[1]

Reaching the age of eighty is a milestone. The realization
of aging is confirmed. My oldest sister often stated that
she did not feel old until her eightieth birthday. At that
point, she could no longer deny that life would not go on

indefinitely. That she, too, was vulnerable to the call of dying. For her, it was those terrible-looking tennis shoes she now had to wear because of the pain in her feet!

Older-old persons have laughed and cried, felt joy and sorrow, lived through pleasure and pain, known love and hatred and been courageous and cringed in fear; despaired in loneliness, suffered losses of family and friends; been delighted with each new birth of a child, and endured difficult, stressful situations.

Each year the awareness of time and space have been gradually altered, enabling a more relativistic attitude toward relationships and toward the importance of events. Feelings are often more easily expressed; actions are understood and conform to individual capabilities.

The perspective of time changes. Keeping oriented to the day of the week may take a conscious, purposeful effort. Weeks and months pass too quickly, days drag by. "Where has the time gone?" A sense of urgency arises as unfinished actions, incomplete business, personal messages, and good intentions push for completion. On the other hand, time seems less important, for the day is sufficient unto itself.

Tomorrow cannot be relied upon as a certainty because something dire may happen, as a misstep may cause a fall and bring disastrous consequences. Plans for future events are made with caution, and an awareness prevails that any plan may not see fruition. "I may die today" is a conscious fearful reality. The process of time passing, of growing older, is characterized by many changes. Each part of our being is affected.

The perspective of space changes. Home becomes too

spacious – too big to take care of the, the lawn too much to mow, too many rooms to keep orderly and clean. The spacious house that seemed so important in earlier years gradually becomes burdensome. To visit children, who perhaps live a distance away, becomes "too much" and hopes rise that children and grandchildren will visit more frequently. Vacations become shorter and less frequent as the desire to see "new places" gives way to the comfort of home.

Space needed for living shrinks. As the older-old consider the future, it was customary to move in with children; now, a move to a smaller house/apartment or a move to an independent living institution are more likely choices. Only thirty percent of the "older-old" remain in the family home although ninety percent would prefer to remain at home. The use of space lessens.

Jack and Jill, married for over forty years, often had tented in parks, and taken a picnic lunch to the nearby forest. Their declining health brought them to an independent living village to live. One day, searching for some variety, they were walking at the local shopping mall. Jack, disabled to some extent by a stroke, bent over and limping along, refused to use a walker. They walked more slowly than usual; Jack became winded, stopped to look at the window display, not sharing his need for breath with Jill. In an instant he fell. The space for a short walk was now too, too far.

Not just our perception of large space, but a more subtle perspective of space affects movements. As we reach to set a glass on the table, we miss by a little inch, spilling its contents on the tablecloth or floor; walking up the stairway, our foot slides off the step and a loss of balance is threatened; reaching to pick up an object from the floor is missed by an inch or two.

The perception of our physical body changes. Physical changes come as early as fifty years of age. The onset of female and male menopause affects our whole being - physical, emotional, and cognitive abilities. Often difficult to accept, and anxiety-provoking, are oncoming signs of differences in physical health, strength, and endurance. Significant adjustments gradually begin, and by sixty-five years, most have experienced a slowing down of activities, moving more slowly, walking carefully, taking a bit longer to perform tasks once done quickly and smoothly, climbing steps causes panting. Driving at night becomes visually difficult. A marked increase in accidents and in falling bring a need for unusual cautiousness and carefulness.

The elderly person is significantly different from the adult person. A precarious balance of health and a predominance of degenerative, rather than reparative body processes gradually develops. An illness or accident may have serious health repercussions, not even predictable from the onset, itself. A minor accident or illness can upset the balance of health and result in a grave illness or severe physical or mental problems. Some physical ailments provide a sudden warning, as in vascular incidents or heart attacks; others creep up exaggerating previous, apparently minor, health events.

Physical movement becomes more difficult – for three-fourths of the older-old have difficulty walking freely. Strength gradually lessens. One elderly man, age 89, expressed frustration that he could no longer reach the upper shelves in the grocery store; he was offended when a younger man offered to help him. Nor could he replace dishes on the second or third shelves; and standing on a two-step stool felt risky.

Physiological changes occur – sometimes gradually, sometimes with warnings as happens with vascular strokes or heart attacks. Functional body systems slow down. Even the process of treatment and recovery from illnesses or diseases are more variable with aging. To quote one medical doctor, "in the elderly duplicity, multiplicity and chronicity tend to be characteristics of symptoms and illnesses."[2]

The Perception of our Self changes: Our personality has a marked consistency throughout life. Five major traits identified by psychologists are: conscientiousness, neuroticism, extroversion, agreeableness, and openness remain quite stable, and define our character.[3] While personality traits do modify in expression from earlier in life, friends and family recognize us by characteristic actions and expressions. With some elderly, character traits become mellowed, softened with growing older; and, with others, traits tend to become hardened, fixed, and rigid.

Unanticipated fears arise. Fears of falling, fears of new or strange situation, fears of dying, or fears of changes in life's patterns. Many fears focus on possible loss of control over one's life or control of events happening about us.

For many, some memory loss occurs, beginning with the loss of names or nouns. Forgetting the name of a good friend, or a recently encountered new person is embarrassing, confusing and irritating.

One 85-year-old lady had a phenomenal memory especially for numbers. She could recall telephone numbers of family members and friends, as well as of doctors, and other business she had to conduct. This was a real benefit until she began confusing numbers. Becoming blind, she gradually lost the visual picture that she used to recall numbers. Fears came. Fears of walking about in her apartment, fears of strangers entering her apartment, fears of new experiences. She sought to remain still and quiet in her familiar home.

Along with these fears are the fearful anticipation of what happens with memory losses. How embarrassing at first to forget a name or a noun. Then, slowly recognizing the problem, the person acknowledges the difficulty, may try humor in acceptance of the loss. Difficulty with perceptual and thought processes may slowly become obvious. Some of this comes with changes in hearing and visual abilities. Reaction time decreases on tasks; learning new material becomes difficult and, the simple act of placing one's foot on the brake to slow the speed of the automobile is takes seconds more. Memory processes change as recalling later experiences predominate over more current activities.

Difficulties with cognitive processes occur. Changes in hearing and visual abilities accentuate thinking difficulties. Reaction time slows when performing tasks; learning new material becomes difficult, and the simple act of placing one's foot on the brake to slow the speed of an automobile requires seconds more. Recalling past experiences now predominates over more current activities.

Problem solving takes more time – time to think; everyday

situations become a little problematic and adjustment to new situations require more time and planning. Yet mental deterioration is not an inevitable function of aging. A focus on the meaning of life becomes prominent, with some turn toward philosophy and spirituality.

Family relationships remain significant to the elderly. Relationships between parents, adult children and grandchildren compel new patterns of interaction. It is often difficult for the older parent to understand the adult child's viewpoint or suggestions and for the adult child to listen to the parents; in turn, the adult child either embraces the wishes and desires of the elderly parent or dis-embraces the parent who has aged, often leaving the parent at a time when the parent needs the intimacy and support provided by the child.

Changing from independence to dependency brings many feelings – shame, anger, sadness, or depression. And within us, there is an increase in aloneness, in loneliness, a decrease in feelings of happiness, a loss of zest for living and eventually a lack of interest in life itself.

I live in an independent living community for senior citizens. The youngest resident is about sixty years of age, the oldest about 106 years. Mary has celebrated her one hundredth birthday. She explained that she would probably live to become 104 years; if still alive then, she would live an additional two years. "And that would be enough." Joe, 97 years old, is a handsome man, a ready smile, and despite a heavy Texan accent, speaks easily and readily with others. Most of his time is given to reading in the library.

Max is 95 years old, an energetic person whose energy has waned since a fall a couple months ago. The fall gave him bruises, but no broken bones. Sports, football, Nascar and especially golf are his main interests. He keeps current with the games, watching television. Helen, 93 years old, moves slowly. Yet she has a mind that is quick, witty and has an intelligence that sparks conversations with thought and knowledge.

These are a few of the imposing persons here on "campus." Mostly all have a pleasant demeanor and positive attitude toward life. They are exceptions to any rule for a normal life, of course, because only about seven percent of those born in 1930 are alive at the age of 85.[4]

I mention these folks briefly so that you, the reader, can understand what makes me react a bit negatively and thoughtfully to research on the lives of persons over seventy-five years. In many studies the older-old are characterized as deficient, failing in both physical and psychological capabilities. The age is described as an age of "psychological mortality bringing a loss of identity, of autonomy and of self-control."[5]

Recognizing that the United State is primarily a youth culture, and no one wishes to grow old, it is disheartening to read that this period of life is the "Disability Zone"[6] because of bio-cultural abilities. Other research reports this is the age of psychological mortality, bringing a loss of identity, of autonomy and of self-control.[7] It is an age of "physical frailty, and of psychological weakness." Others emphasize the desire for new information declines: "Information literacy skills diminish as individuals do not keep in touch with the technological advances required in the present day." Attention to events in the community and/or nation wane significantly, objective information rarely concerns the aging person. Finally, another view, a bit more political is the older-old are a burden to society with tremendous cost because of the need for physical, medical, and economic care. As one researcher questioned whether these oldest-old years" reduces the opportunities of an increasing number to ...die with dignity."[8]

As the reader may realize, the individual person is not considered in much research. The strengths, capabilities, feelings are deemed of less important. It is my hope to provide a discussion and guidelines to ease some difficulties encountered and to recognize the strengths that enables long living. Finally, to share the admiration, awe, and understanding of the wonders of log life. My focus is on the desires and needs, the sense of gratitude and help for the process of adjustment to increasing age.

Maslow, a psychologist writing in the 1950's, outlined a hierarchy of five areas of requirement for living that provides a guideline for us.[9] These are: (1) Care for our physical needs; (2) Assurance of security and safety; (3) Attachment to others, belongingness and love needs; (4) Feelings of accomplishment and self-esteem; and (5) A sense of self-actualization. Later a sixth was added – that of having a sense of meaning in life.

The following chapters are devoted to requisites for the older-old to age successfully and gracefully. Let us now look at the basic need for all – the need for physical life support and emotional security.

REFERENCES

1. For these statistics, please refer to: Arias, E., Heron M. Xu JQ., U.S. Department of Health and Human Services. National Vital Statistics Reports: vol 66 no. 3 Hyattsville, MD. National Center for Health Statistics, April 2017.

2. J.W. Beattie. "Elderly life: Its Characteristics, Needs and Philosophy," J College. Gen Practit. 2963,6,20.

3. Digman, JM (1990) "Personality Structure. Emergence of the five-factor model" Annual Review of Psychology. 41.417-440

4. Arias, F., Heron, M., Xu JG. (2017) United States Life Tables. National vital statistics reports. Vol. 66 No. 3. Hyattsville, MD National Center for Health Statistics.

5. Many ideas for this section are from Dr. Habil. Jacqui Smith. (2000) "The Fourth Age: A Period of Psychological Mortality?" the Max Planck Institute for Human Development, Berlin and the Research Group of Psychological Gerontology, Department of Psychiatry, Medical School, Free University, Berlin

6. Baltes, P.S., Smith, J. (2003) "New Frontiers in the Future of Aging: From Successful Aging of the Young Old to the Dilemmas of the Fourth Age" Gerontology 2003:49:123-135.

7. ASLA, T., WILLIAMSON, KK., & MILLS, J. (2006): THE ROLE OF INFORMATION IN: THE CASE FOR A RESEARCH FOCUS ON THE OLDEST OLD: LIBRARY & INFORMATION SCIENCE RESEARCH 28(1) 49-63.

8. Almak, P. (2002) "Death with Dignity" Journal of Medical Ethics 28:255-257.

9. MASLOW, A. H. (1987) MOTIVATION AND PERSONALITY (3RD EDITION) DELHI, INDIA. PEARSON EDUCATION.

CHAPTER THREE

A Home For Growing Older

As we rock back and forth on the ocean of joys and woes of life, home is a place of safety and security. Home is our rock, our base for living. Here are people we love, things we cherish, and memories we remember. Some things are still cherished, others worn out by use; memories accumulate within us. Children drift away, afloat on their own sea. Home no longer provides security we need; old age has settled upon us.

TO FIND A HOME

Uncertainty floods the thoughts of older people when contemplating the future. What may befall them? Where shall we live? How can we care for ourselves? How to plan effectively? Is it possible, yea even necessary, to find a home better suited for our unpredictable future? Should we stay here? What would that entail? How may we arrange for necessary care? Is now a good time to plan? How to retain our dignity? A search for safety begins.

A dire situation arises when an illness or disability compels immediate action to find a desirable place. If there have been no contingency plans, a choice of living situation becomes stress ridden. Investigation of choices and selection of an appropriate place for the family member becomes a hasty, even desperate search. It is really preferable to plan before the necessity demands.

A desire for contentment, satisfaction, and peace with life becomes especially important. Hope prevails to end life's path with safety and security. Safety refers to absence of fears and apprehension in physical and environmental surrounds. Emotional security refers to a sense confidence and freedom from apprehension.[1] Seniors seek the safety of knowing that physical needs -including illnesses or disabilities – will receive excellent medical care and physical comfort. They dread the idea of facing illnesses alone or without good care. They seek a place to alleviate these concerns in the best way possible. Emotional challenges encountered are often more severe than in earlier times – for life and death are constant concerns. Primary needs, as the assurance for sustenance, health, safety, and security, now take precedence. At first look, these seem givens in our culture. But the realization that forty-eight per cent of older people subsist financially below the national poverty level, it becomes obvious that many lacks enough nurturance.[2]

How do senior citizens decide to change home?

Jack (75 years) and Rita (72) have lived in their home over forty years. They have loved their home and community.

Their three children grew up and went to school from here. With pleasant memories embedded in the walls of the house, they were reluctant to leave "home", to find another. Jack, aged 76, had suffered heart ailments during the last years. Now, with decreasing energy, he was not able to manage the care of the house or perform those chores he once loved. It was time to find a home more adapted to his and his wife's physical capabilities. This is a common story of many older persons faced with problems of managing for their home or finding a new one.

About eighty percent of persons of sixty-five years of age state they would prefer to remain in their current home for the rest of their lives[3]; only forty-six percent think it will be possible.[4] While some health and nurturance services are offered for home care by state and federal resources, they are insufficient to provide for the growing numbers of aging citizens. Unable to feel safe in their home, the elder person is often compelled to find a place to live that provides for their oncoming needs. A free choice becomes more difficult when the person is compelled by acute physical and/or cognitive problems that involve assisted care.

WHAT CONSIDERATIONS LEAD TO A DESIRE FOR MORE CONVENIENT LIVING SITUATION?

There are many reasons for finding a more appropriate home place. While the motivation for moving differs for individuals, the reasons cluster around the following:

The onset or fear of health problems or increasing disability:

Persons seventy-five years and older have an average of two chronic health problems not including visual, hearing or dental problems.[5] With health difficulties comes increasing dependence on others for everyday activities, including personal care. No one accepts a loss of self-reliance easily. Home and independence are valued as long as possible. Many are reluctant to accept that they need help. It is difficult to make a move that indicates a reliance on someone or something else.

Example: Bob, age 78, had suffered two strokes – the first blinding him in one eye, the second affecting his walking. He was compelled to use a walker, even to get around at home. With responsibility for the care Bob required, His wife, Jane, found it increasingly difficult to care for Bob and to manage the household chores. They looked for an independent living community in which home and medical care were assured.

Problems with thinking and memory: Increasing memory problems or thinking abilities bring feelings that it may be better to act "now" than await more serious situations. An increasing need for help brings an awareness that a change of residence is desirable and permits time to select a living environment both desirable and suitable.

Instance: Fred and Jane had been married twenty years, the second marriage for both. Fred had developed his own company from humble beginnings to a successful international corporation. Louise was the mother of four children and had been mother to Fred's children as well. The ease of living gradually disappeared. Louise suffered from diabetes, Fred, always a precise and careful person, had become preoccupied with details. He would spend much time tightening the five hundred screws on the garage door (which he had counted) so it would not fall apart. Also, after driving a mile or two from home, he would often be compelled to return to home, anxiety and agitated. He felt compelled to check if he had locked the garage doors. These were oft repeated behaviors. His compulsive behaviors were interfering with the simplicity of living. Fears of dementia clouded the future. Aware that his anxiety and fears were becoming overwhelming, they decided that a move to an assisted living home in which medical and psychological was available, would provide care for his anxiousness and give both security.

Nearness to children or relatives. Children have often settled a distance from their family home, having moved due to employment or other reasons. Now, as parents are aging, the parents are faced with a desire to live closer to their children -and grandchildren – to keep the emotional closeness of family relationships. And, of course, the probability of giving and receiving help is important to parents and children. The change of residence itself brings stress for the parents as well as stress on the child(ren) as they adjust to the nearness and possible dependency of the parents. Generally, this works out well, with both homes making an adequate adjustment to the changes that the move brings. While both parties enjoy the environmental closeness, life is variable and inconstant as has been the case many times.

The fluctuations of life may cause difficult changes even after the family seems settled and safe. Adult children with their families may be compelled to move away through instances of job transfers, or other forces in their living.

Example: Bob and Jean had chosen a desirable retirement home in New Mexico some distance from their children. They had three children, all married and with children of their own. As Bob and Jean grew older, the children seemed too far away to visit or be visited easily by their children and families. They moved to the same city as the children and settled in an apartment smaller than their former home. All seemed well until the oldest son was moved by his employer to another state; then, within another year, the second family also moved. Now, seemingly caught by "fate's" accidents, the family was separated again. This distressful story is not unusual. There are unpredictable events in life that challenge any plan.

The home is ill-adapted to the aging persons. A home selected in earlier life may not be adapted to the requirements of an aging person. Unnoticed and unimportant when the home was first purchased, were the steps required to enter the house, the steps to climb to the upper or lower sections, no safety bars for bathrooms, no carpeting to provide assurance against slipping and falling. Remodeling of features of the home would be needed for safety and security. Also, the upkeep of the house itself, such as the need for a new roof, cleaning the garage, fixing the roof and/or for an onset of additional expenses as taxes, becomes difficult.

Loss of independence: For many seniors, the inability to care for themselves and for a home comes gradually. The Encore Phase brings increasing dependence on others. Whether it involves depending on others for physical care of an aging person, as in bathing, dressing, eating, etc. or with care of the home as with chores in preparing meals, cleaning the house (and electric sweepers are often heavy) washing or ironing, all become increasingly difficult and burdensome. The loss of independence comes with normal aging processes.

Example: A couple, Grace and Edward, at ages 74 and 80, were active physically, still playing tennis and golf. They had lived in their home for over thirty years. When asked what happened that led them to think of moving, Edward responded that the lawn was too large for him to mow, the roof of the house needed replacement, the bathroom and kitchen needed remodeling, windows needed recaulking, etc. Grace, ill with diabetes, gladly agreed. His parents had waited until they were compelled to move because of disabilities and illnesses. This brought much stress on Grace and Edward. Now, they wanted to take of themselves and their future while they were able and not be a burden to their children.

The freedom of mobility and movement lessens: For many seniors, the loss of the freedom of movement threatens the core of one's being. Losing license to drive a car erases an ability to manage important errands, as grocery shopping, going to doctor appointments, visiting friends, driving to church, etc. More crushing to the spirit is a loss of ability to walk freely. Reliance on a cane, a walker or even wheelchair compels a new examination of life. Ability to utilize space has diminished.

An increasing sense of vulnerability brings a need for environmental security. Neighborhoods pass through important changes over the years, such as the depreciation of homes or neighborhood. A loss of independence brings a need for environmental security.

Social and Community preferences

The location of a new residence is important for promoting and enabling social interaction. Interaction with others is a major factor that contributes to a better quality of life. When neighborhood relationships have developed over time, the community that is formed, although informal, often provide some sustenance and care for each other. In our mobile society, supportive neighborhood relationships seldom have the time to form inter-supportive bonding.

Another aspect of the environment concerns the environment that one desires. For instance, some independent communities are cloistered, far from stores, commerce, buses, medical car and/or other city amenities. This provides a cloistered, peaceful setting; or it may be considered too isolated for some who prefer a "city-like" environment and choose to remain part of the busy-ness of life.

Being able to walk about in a neighborhood without fear and enjoy one's neighbors and community is important. Communities change over the years and a once congenial neighborhood may be affected through economic downturns and become quite unpleasant. Or, to the contrary, the neighborhood may be "renovated", housing prices increase, and community may provide a financial boost.

Example: Edward and Grace, who were previously

discussed, noted changes in their neighborhood that affected their decision to move. They observed that after twenty-five years of living in their home, the neighborhood had changed; there was no longer children laughing and playing in front lawns, or neighbors sitting on the front porch. Once a neatly kept environment, the general aging of the neighborhood over twenty years had now lessened a sense safety. The once well-kept neighborhood had gradually changed; several homes had suffered "break-ins": lawns were not mowed, etc. This loss of safety is important for the person of any age, but with age comes an increasing awareness of vulnerability and lessening ability protect themselves.

Example: An incidence I well remember shook me to the core. A friend, Mary, aged 84, lived alone in an apartment situated in a middle-class community where she had many friends and knew her neighbors well. One day, she volunteered to baby-sit for a friend. With the baby asleep, she was relaxing. Sitting on the porch, she was accosted by a stranger, a man, who forced her into the apartment and then raped her. While basically in a "safe" environment, she had not been safe enough. Although preferring to remain in her apartment of many years, her decision to move to an independent community where physical safety was more assured came immediately after this incident.

Then there are more personal reasons for wishing to find a new home. These are many and are relative to the person, but among the more common reasons are:

Aloneness and vulnerability. The loss of partner, family and friends increases a sense of aloneness. About thirty per cent of older adults over 65 years live alone; over 85 years of age, about fifty percent live alone, over half are women over 75 years.[6] Not all make the choice of moving to a more social community, preferring the independence of living alone. While being alone may at times be preferred, the loneliness that may set in becomes unbearable. Despair and hopelessness may immobilize the person. Often enough, a depression comes and overwhelms an impetus for life.

Being alone increases fears of vulnerability – no one near enough to care, to respond in in a needful time, or to be present. Many, who remain alone in the community in which she had lived many years, suffer an increase in loneliness and withdrawal further, even from contact with her friends and neighbors. Others, wanting to avoid loneliness, seek a more socially oriented environment.

Example: Mary, aged 85, had been living alone since her husband died twenty years ago. Even though she was wealthy, she lived alone and without any help in the home she and her husband had built. Her housekeeper cleaned only her bedroom; the rest of the house was "closed up." She was bedfast, living in her bed and bedroom. She could not walk without the help of a walker or wheelchair; she crawled to the bathroom. One day, trying to help her in any way she might accept, I asked her if she read, and would she like some books. She responded, "I do not read." Imagine my surprise soon after when I saw several printed pamphlets addressing complex financial affairs on her bed! What she meant was that she did not entertain herself with reading; the pamphlets provided important information for her welfare. Mary wanted the freedom of being alone to the end in her own home, risking the absence of medical care and nutrition she needed. Incidentally, she kept open carton of Ensure on her bed.

Financial considerations: There are financial costs to be considered in remaining in the home and in changing residence. Most people will need help in looking at their financial status, for the cost of staying and/or of moving entail expenditures that may be difficult to predict. Seeking professional advice may be important before any decision is made.[7]

Compelled by children's wishes. There are times when the children take the initiative and move the parent without the parents' agreement or consent. The motivation of the children may be a sincere caring for the parent, a disregard for the needs of the parent, or even an action of hostility. Changes of residence, no matter the motive, are especially stress-ridden for the parent, and often are followed by a downturn in the parent's health. Perhaps the parent has suffered disability or illness and now requires more care that the children can provide.

In cases of moderate to severe dementia of the parent, the children may feel compelled to provide a safe environment for the parent and consider the parent is unable to understand or accept the change. Hopefully in such instances, the change has been discussed carefully with the parent so that she/he at least has some understanding of the reasons.

Many a parent becomes submissive to the will of the child, foregoing any request or statement of his/her own choice. "Whatever you think is best" shows a reliance on the will of the child, passively accepting a child's decisions, trusting in good-will, or fearful of desertion by the child.

Example: One man whose spouse had died years before, relied and trusted the eldest of three children who lived closest to him. Because of partial blindness, he had asked his son for help with money matters, as paying the monthly bills. The son decided the father should move closer to him; he selected an independent living community, which, he stated to a sister, was "not very nice" and he, himself, would never go there. The father, fearful of expressing his preference for a different community, accepted the son's recommendation. The repercussions were disastrous for the parent, compelled to live in a "not-so-nice place" and losing control over his finances as the son expanded his self-assumed duties. It is a caring, loving gesture toward an aging parent when supportive children and aged parent can discuss these matters. *If at all possible*, the choice should be made by the aged parent.

In my work with families, I have become aware of several older persons who moved into a residential community because of the pressure of children. One memorable instance occurred when a mother had been living with a son and his family for a couple years. Following the son's divorce, and with the help of siblings, mother was moved to an independent living apartment. On the day of the move, she was told this was her new home. She had not known she was moving alone, thinking she was moving to her son's new home. This move was not her wish, nor was the move discussed in a way that the mother was prepared for the traumatic impact of a strange home and aloneness. The adult children had made the decision without the concurrence of the parent. Family pressures are highly individualized and result from a historicity of family relationships and interactions as well as from a concern for the parent's health and welfare.

WHAT ARE THE AVAILABLE OPTIONS FOR CHANGING RESIDENCE?

These considerations reflect the problems that many elderly persons face as they think of moving. Each of these reasons is enough to be a motivation for changing home. Often enough it is not one factor, but several that must be considered.

Many are reluctant to leave the familiarity and security of their long-term family home. Memories from the family home linger. An inevitable comparison of the lost home to the new lingers. The nostalgia and color of memories shade the acceptance of the new home. There are several options open for seniors wanting a safe, secure and health-oriented home place. The following are possibilities to be considered in a decision to move.

Remaining at home: In the United States, twelve million or about 26 per cent of seniors over the age of 65 live alone in their home. Seventy-nine percent are women; eighteen percent are men.[8] About sixty per cent of persons over 65 have lived in their home for twenty years, three-fourths state they would prefer to remain there. They choose to rely on community services that are available, specifically, home care services for medical necessities and/or a program like "meals on wheels" for daily food.

Living with children or other family members: About eight per cent of older parents would prefer to live with family members. And there is an increase in the number of adult children living with their parents and of parents moving in with adult children.[9]

Senior Housing. There are apartments or condominiums within many communities that are areas designed for people over age 5 who can live independently. These apartments seldom provide meals or personal care services of any kind, although security personnel may be present.

Independent living community. In the past twenty years, many independent living communities designed for senior citizens have been built. They usually consist of homes or apartments that are maintenance free, and furnished by the residents. Services vary with the community. Some provide 24-hour security, a community center, fitness center and other types of services. Health care is available or may be purchased from available sources. Daily check-ins are available in most communities. Activities, as movies, programs, educational opportunities are usually available.

Assisted living Centers: Residents of assisted living communities suffer disabilities or illnesses that make independent living and self-care difficult. These communities usually provide three meals a day, within a common dining area, and aid that is needed – such as laundry and housekeeping, self-care as bathing, dressing, and professional care for managing medications. Usually security staff are present, and other staff are available around the clock. An assisted living or rehabilitation center may be a short-term placement while the person recovers from an illness or disability and may then return home.

Assisted living centers often include a rehabilitation center. This may be a temporary placement for persons are referred here for occupational and/or physical therapy along with nutritional care, to aid recovery from an accident or illness. When the person needs more full-time care, there are specialized assistant living centers in which the level of service is adapted to the needs of the person.

Nursing Care Centers:

Other kinds of communities

Memory Care: These centers provide services specific to Alzheimer's disease and memory losses. They offer twenty-four supervised care in a structured environment. Usually, active therapy and behavioral management services are available. These are units within centers for assisted living or independent living centers. They are designed to provide the specific help required by dementia and/or Alzheimer's diseases. These centers strive to help residents keep as much independence as possible.

Hospice Care. Full 24-hour care may be required with a terminal illness. There are special units that provide medical, nursing and physical care.

III. HOW CAN I MAKE THE BEST CHOICE? SUGGESTIONS FOR AN APPROACH

The idea of moving may have developed gradually throughout a couple years, watching friends leave or move. The decision comes with some anguish for there is not only the trauma of leaving home and its family history behind, but also the anxiety of finding a new place and of the process of moving itself. For the senior citizen, changing a home subtracts more energy and health than at earlier ages.

It is well accepted that moving is among the top three sources of stress and anxiety at any age, and a greater stress for the older citizen. The move should be made with as much care as possible. First is a selection of place —at a time when physical reserves are not as great as once were. A look at the reasons for moving let us know that any or all the reasons may pertain. For those over 75 years, it is often a traumatic step, especially if the move comes with the onset of a disability or illness. The following are suggestions for problem-solving that were first described by Baltes in recognizing how many elderly actually approach difficulties. It is described in the literature as the Selection-Optimization-Compensation (SOC) method.[10]

Investigation: The first step is to recognize reasons for a change, and then discuss the type of community that has the optimal care needed. The investigation and the process of selection is a topic to be shared with the family. The decision remains with the senior citizens for theirs is the life that is changing. The first task is to determine the safety, comfort and service necessary. What is desired in a new residence? What medical or health care services would be needed?

Other questions may be: Will this be a pleasant place to call home? Do you wish for a city environment with those amenities nearby? Or do you prefer a quieter, place with some nature surrounding? Do you prefer a biophilic design? Are the rooms a suitable size? What household tasks would you need/want such as house cleaning, laundry of clothes, of sheets and towels, etc. What food services are desired? Do you prefer that a good restaurant be available? Will you need help with transportation, now or in the future -such as transportation to medical care, grocery shopping, etc.? What availability of outdoors, parks, etc., is available – if it preferred?

What connection to the community is desirable...the isolation within a community is an often-heard complaint? Are programs of entertainment and/or education available? Are excursions off the "campus" provided?

Selection. Now that possible residences have been identified, compare the services offered by each with the services desired. Consideration of health needs are granted the highest priority. Which offer the physical care that is needed. What kind of physical, rehabilitation programs are present? What additional services would be desirable – a library, a social program, educational opportunities? Are the room sizes acceptable? Then, the environment – do you want to be in a city, or a calm and peaceful environment? Usually there will favorable and not-so-favorable situations with any choice.

Try to list the selections in order of desirability. Then

consider how each community provides the services in your list and what is lacking.

Optimization: Optimization refers to making the choice best possible. It requires an exploration of stimulating and enhancing programs provided. The question is, how can the adaptation to the new home be improved through the services offered. The elderly often suffers from lack of environmental stimulation; it is important to know additional opportunities are included for enriching life. And, what possibilities are there for additional activities or stimulating new interests?

Compensation: Compensation involves providing alternate means to manage any difficulties the selection may bring. Seldom is there a perfect answer for all problems. What are the available alternate choices for both physical and social activities? It may require learning new skills such as the use of computers or technological processes, or even how to use "smart telephones" to maintain contact visually as well as auditorily with family and friends. Compensation may even require receiving help from others, such as a companion; it may involve planning for a driver, if one no longer drives; or use of a hearing aid, when hearing fails. It is a process of responding to what is missing, before it missed, if possible. In this way, problems may be eased, possibly before they appear.

These are three essential processes for problem solving. What is necessary? required? What is needed for enrichment of life? How to attend to personal interests and desires and needs? The final considerations revolve around personal reactions. Which place did you like? In which setting did you feel most accepted? In which setting would you feel most comfortable, most at home? In which setting will you feel most likely to invite friends? In which setting will you most enjoy? The choice will ultimately be an emotional choice, a place where you will feel satisfied, most content. The selection then made is chosen to provide the most contentment and pleasure.

Important in this process is this: When presented with any difficult problem, *the elder citizen adjusts better when he/ she has made the decision.*

The primary needs for life include a safe home, a secure environment and sufficient nurturance. Elder citizens ultimately encounter insecurity about the satisfaction of these needs. Planning permits confidence that life and care will be supplied. The confidence may come from family members or from services guaranteed by the chosen residence.

Homeward bound, a place of refuge for the storms ahead, a place for the heart to be calmed, for the soul to find grace as the end of life's journey.

PART II. THE JOY AND AGONY OF RELOCATION

Turbulence is in the winds of the move. Although well planned, the vicissitudes of the events now to be weathered required a lightness of the spirit, an acceptance of the unexpected, time that was not planned, unexpected moods, and curiosity for newness.

Effects of moving

Changing one's home is identified as one of the most stressful events faced by young and old persons alike.[11] Leaving a home and moving to another requires a resilience to the frustrations, mix-ups, or misunderstandings that seem to pop out of nowhere - that interfere with the anticipated excitement or enjoyment of the day. It has been well established that relocation is stressful. Several negative physical reactions, as increased mortality, and psychological reactions, as a decline in perceived control over life events, are common. The lack of control, both before and after a move, is a primary factor.[12]

Frustrations of a new residence may include such mundane events and feelings as: *Finding* those things in the new home: Where did I put that? Did I remember to bring that? What did I do with it? *Orientation* to the new home: as awakening in a new bedroom – where am I? *Old habits* don't work, new ones change the usual sequence of the day; even the clothes are in a different place; what am I doing next? What is the neighborhood like? How will I ever get used to this place? Where is the cafeteria? When do I eat? The food is not what I usually have. Where is the post office? Where can I buy a toothbrush?

There have been several research efforts studying the effects of changing homes.[13] A most important factor that emerges is the degree of control that the older person has upon the transfer. When pushed by others or other circumstances, the older persons is stressed not only by the move, but by the loss of control of life. This failure of making important life situations may increase the effects of stress.

When planning beforehand, control of time of move, and predictability of changing home site has occurred, it is easier to accept the new home and adapt to its environment. The first reaction, aside from the excitement and agitation of moving itself, is to recognize that there will be a time of sadness, even depression, after leaving a home where one has resided for some time. This sadness turns into a nostalgia for what has been given up, and the nostalgia becomes memories. A balance of the pleasant and unpleasant memories is retained.

When the move was initiated by the elderly person, and there has been thoughtful and careful preparation, the relocation is less stressful. The new environment then encourages an open exploration and curiosity of new environs, new persons one meets, and programs and services available.

When the older person has been poorly adjusted prior to the move, such as being socially isolated, living alone, or depressed, the adjustment is difficult.[14] This is especially so if there has been a minimum of preparation. With inadequate preparation, the individual sacrifices the ability to predict, to know what happens next, to feel secure. It takes much effort to reach out to the new, to feel confident, to take steps to acquaint one's self to the new setting. Avoidance sets in, except for requirements of the new environment. Without some help, the isolation or depression often increases.

Moving from one institutional setting to another often indicates the need for different quality of care for the person. Other considerations may be family nearness, financial difficulties or parent's wishes. The person is given little control over the change unless there is careful preparation. Often the ability of the present institution is not prepared to offer the service needed; the option is movement to another more appropriate. Even in these situations, the re-adjustment by elderly persons is dependent on the person's sense of choice and of awareness of the new setting. Further, sudden, unexpected transfers are traumatic. One study reported that over twenty-thousand elderly persons that were transferred from one setting to another, about thirty-two percent died within one year of the transfer.[15] Any move can have physical and psychological affects for those in acute or long-term care. Often sudden or unexpected change may bring depression, irritability, exacerbation of illness and elevated mortality rate.

CONCLUSIONS

Home is the place where you feel in control and properly oriented in space and time; it is a predictable and secure place. The search for a home for the ending of life has caused many elderly persons to abandon a home of many years for a place that will take care of the increasing challenges of the later years of life. There are three factors that are essential in a successful adjustment to changing homes. First: *The greater the choice the individual has, the less negative the effects of relocation.* That is, the elderly person who is making the change of residence will adapt better if he/she selects the new home. Second: *the principle of predictability.* The more familiar the new environment is, the more predictable the new environment is, the less negative the effects of moving. Third: *the principle of control.* Having some control over choices, over timing of the move, etc., is a way in which individuals cope with a stress situation. Without some control over events, the stress is magnified and the stress reactions more debilitating.

REFERENCES

1. See "security" a definition given by N.Pam M.S., "Security" in PsychologicalDictionary.org, April 26, 2013, (accessed Oct. 4, 2019.

2. Cubanski, J., Kome, W., Neuman, I. Damico, A. (Nov. 19, 2018) "How many seniors live in poverty?" 2019. San Francisco, CA. Kaiser Family Foundation.

3. These statistics are from the Joint Center for Housing Studies of Harvard University, "Meeting the Needs of an Aging Population" Also see "Most Retirees Prefer to stay put" in Planning for Retirement, AARP Bulletin (/bulletin/) October 10, 2018.

4. Most Retirees prefer to stay at home. Please see "Planning for Retirement". AARP Bulletin (/bulletin/) October 10, 2018

5. By 2005, the percentage of older adults had increased to 91 percent. See The National Institute on Aging, Department of Health and Human Resources

6. (Merck Manual: Professional Version 2018 Merck Sharp & Dohme Corp., Kenilworth NJ Older Adults Living Alone by Daniel B. Kaplan and Barbara J. Berkman)

7. This is a topic of immense significance. It was not the aim of this book to provide specific information on finances. Instead, the reader is referred to the many organizations that provide specific help for retirement planning. Please refer to publications of The National Council of Aging.

8. "By the Numbers: Older Adults living Alone." American Psychological Associations, May 2016, Vol. 47, No. 5 (American Psychological Association.

9. "More Older Adults are moving in with their children? http:AARP/Winter/aarp.org. February 5, 2018.

10. This method was first described by Paul b\Bates in 1990. The present selection is from: Freund, Alexandra M. and Baltes, Paul B. "Selection, optimization and compensation as strategies of life management: Correlations with subjective indicators of successful aging" (1998/12. The American Psychological Association in

Psychology and Aging, Vol. 13. No. 4

11. Neal, Brandi. "Moving is one of the Most Stressful Life Events, A new Study Reports" September 7, 2015.

12. Jackson, Kate. "Prevent Elder Transfer Trauma: Tips to Ease Relocation Stress" January/February 2015 Issue. Social Work Today

13. Ewen, Heidi H. (2013) "Influence of Late Life Stressors on the Decisions of Older Women to Relocate into Congregate Senior Housing. H Hous Elderly Oct 1: 27(4): 392-408.

14. Kaplan, B. Donald, Berkman, Barbara J. "Effects of Life Transitions on Older Adults" May 2019. Merck manual, Merck. Sharp and Dohne Corp., Inc. Kenilworth NJ.

15. Danermark, Berth D., Ekstrom, Mats E. and Bodin, Lenhart L. "Effects of residential relocation on morality and morbidity among elderly People>"

CHAPTER FOUR

The Positivity Of Aging

The ocean has calmed, the waves delicately move the waters...a beautiful, rhythmic flow...off in the distance there is a surge of water coming, clouding the blue sky's blessings...... waiting for the turbulence....it will come...and destroy the beautiful peace...and overwhelms the peacefulness...

INTRODUCTION:

Thus is life in this period. There are times of calmness, beautiful times to reflect on life, to live it even more fully with delight in each day that brings no pain...this time is a gift...a time to enjoy living, to enjoy life as it is. On the horizon lies a mostly unknowable end. Yes, life's end becomes nearer each day. Time is ours ...to live. We hug it.

Some days wake us with a smile, just feeling good and happy...looking to whatever the day may bring. Sometimes the wakening moments are slow, gradually we peruse the day, wondering what it will bring, for our body-self carries us through those automatic acts of fixing and eating breakfast, cleaning up the dishes, and any acts that follow. Here we are, nothing special looms to color the day. It is a good day. We like time for ourselves. Sometimes a few exercises feel good and brighten the mood for the day.

Yet another day, we awaken with ennui, nothing special is happening, life is on an even keel. Other greet each day with an emptiness, wondering how to find a life through another un-special day. The day feels endless.

Our manner of greeting the day reflects who we are... those unique constellations of emotions, behaviors, attitudes, and thoughts; that collection of traits that characterize us, our personality. Personality consists of inherent propensities, of the quality of nurturing received, of the impact of special events upon our feelings, thinking and behavior throughout life, and of implicit cultural expectations. A continuity of personality persists throughout life.

Have we changed with age?

It is a common assumption that personality shows a continuity of characteristics over the life span. Meeting longtime friends after many years of absence, they recognize us by familiar traits, expressions, and behavior. "Oh, I remember how you used to do that!" While time and experience may bring change, basic traits remain the same, though tendered by effects and experiences of life's events.

Are we the same persons? Yes and no. Yes, the experiences of time and physical changes have altered some but not those lasting characteristics, not our self. Yes, we still have that stubborn or shy child within, and that child even now takes over some times. Yes, we are still reluctant to join a new group; yes, we still prefer others to speak. Yes, we still become angered when someone interrupts a story.

No, we are quite different. When we reflect on the differences, we even feel the change. No longer the shy child, we speak up to defend ourselves or to present an opposing view. That feels different; it feels strong even though when we first tried it, it was frightening.

We can be firm, even angry, in a manner that would have frightened the child. No, we do not speak as quickly, nor behave quite as impulsively, as we might have during adolescence, we have learned not to address our superiors in the same manner we talked to our parents. We bite our tongue to remain silent at times. We no longer inflict personal attitudes and beliefs on others that might spoil the mood of conversation. We practice patience and tolerance with other persons and ideas.

Yes and no, we are the same and different. Experiences have brought a refinement of behavior. In many instances, we adjust our behavior, not always our feelings, to meet the expectations of others. We also become aware that others react differently, and others feel and think differently. Alterations of attitudes and behaviors demonstrate growth of personhood. Characteristic constellations of thought, emotion, and behavior mark the individualization of the person. It appears to be relatively stable throughout our life, specifically from adolescence throughout adulthood. For example, in experiences of meeting a long-absent childhood friend, there is an almost a spontaneous remembering "how" that person was and still is. "You always..." are common phrases used to renew the friendship. We know, we feel within us the continuity of our being; we sense ourselves as the same person, with changes taking place within us. The core of our being is here.

The relative stability of personality has been observed through research, beginning in 1918, with the research of Lewis Terman at Stanford University. They followed the lives of about 2,000 gifted children.[1] Using the results of interviews with teachers, parents, the subjects themselves, and tests of personality and intelligence, he identified five basic traits of personality: (1) openness to experience – a curiosity, and imagination; (2) conscientiousness – patterns of organization, productiveness and responsibility; (3) extraversion - including sociability and assertiveness, or the opposite, introversion and timidity; (4) agreeableness - including compassion, respectfulness and trust in others or fixed ideas and attitudes, questioning and distrust; and, (5) stability of moods – as emotionally well-balanced, stable, and composed - opposite as in neuroticism, anxiety and depressions. The studies followed the children, parents, even the grandchildren, and continued, at least, until 1991.

Does the personality remain stable, do emotions and behavior change throughout life? Which characteristics last? Terman's, and other studies that followed, showed that cheerfulness, high motivation, or sociability predict reduced longevity[2]. Conscientiousness was one characteristic identified in childhood studies that was clearly related to survival to old age.

There are hints that emotional stability may be associated with longevity among males (i.e., neuroticism may be unhealthy) and that conscientiousness may be weaker among females than among males. Anxiousness or fearfulness, and childhood hyperactivity color adult adjustment, lead to increased physical problems, and thus earlier aging.

Observing a group of elder persons interact, the variety of personalities is remarkable. There is Jane, who talks incessantly; Susan, who is quiet, speaking only when addressed; Mari, adding to the topic of any conversation; Jean, who always seems angry about something; Phoebe, who seems to be the leader for everyone listens to her; and, Larry, whose voice always demands attention, etc., etc., These are not persons sharing obvious personality traits. Yet each in their own way speak of life as fulfilling, with a sense of contentment, and are pleased with life.

THE POSITIVITY OF AGEING – HOW DOES IT AFFECT ONE?

Emotional well-being seems pervasive among the oldest-old. There is a positive glow to life. – a sense of well-being. How is this possible? Well-being refers to the balance between positive and negative feelings - involving happiness, satisfaction with life, and contentment. Notable among the oldest-old is an increase in the sense of well-being throughout aging until poor health or disability quietens the life spirit.

Over the past few years, research has shown that older

people are more likely to remember events and stimuli that are emotionally meaningful and pleasant to them. This effect has been termed the "positivity effect." Attending to and remembering what is positive, rather than negative, is a relative preference among older people compared to younger adults. Scores of studies from multiple laboratories, utilizing a wide variety of methodological approaches, have shown that older adults give more attention and remember positive better than negative information. For instance, this pattern is revealed when a series of pictures are shown to persons of different ages, or when lists of emotionally loaded words, or when situational descriptions are described – the items evoking positive feelings are remembered more frequently.[3] Carstensen suggests that positivity is an adaptive process for everyday living for the aging person. It is the result of reflection, and of controlled thinking, of the present situation, and the sense of time in life.[4]

Positivity is reflected in everyday interactions. When an older person is asked, "how are you today?" The response is often, "fine." One friend, John, 85 years old and a retired captain of a merchant ship, will always say he is feeling fine. His answer is readily given even though his physical disabilities are observable. However, when his back is painful, the answer is more dire – he smirks, salutes and comments, "I am here" and limps on his way.

This pattern is not the result of an aging brain. Positivity has been demonstrated to depend on the availability of cognitive resources. It vanishes when cognitive resources are relatively meager, as in Alzheimer's disease or dementia. When attention is divided, and the person must attend to a task at hand, the positivity gives way to the action required. In research, when comparing the emotional memory of younger, of older adults and of older adults suffering from Alzheimer's disease, those with Alzheimer's remembered a greater proportion of negative versus positive words than the other two groups.[5] Positivity seems to be lost, to disappear, when cognitive disabilities are present. Positivity serves to enhance decision-making and problem-solving events especially when related to the well-being of the person. It facilitates adaptation to choices and problems that arise.

Positivity reflects many aspects of the aging person.[6] Aware that time for life is limited, the older person makes choices that are emotionally gratifying.

EMOTION IN THE SUMMING UP AND ENCORE PERIOD

Emotional life is relatively unaffected by aging and often improves with age, especially in emotional problem solving.[7] Some emotional reactions, as the ability to recognize and react to others' feelings may decline with age.

Basic, or primary, emotions come with being human. The recognition of primary emotions is part of human history, dating back to the *Book of Rites*, a first century Chinese encyclopedia. It identifies seven "feelings of men": joy, anger, sadness, fear, love, disliking and liking. In present day psychology, eight basic emotions have been suggested as universally experienced in all human cultures.[8] These are: joy, trust, fear, surprise, sadness, anticipation anger and distrust. With experience of life, these feelings expand, becoming mixed and complex as more than one emotion is evoked at a time. Most of us are familiar with joy, cheerfulness, enthusiasm, laughter, curiosity, pride, hope apathy grief, guilt, despair, regret, shame, etc. Each is a fusion of basic emotions, brought about by feelings evoked from with us, or stimulated from an outer situation. There are now over seven thousand facial expressions recognized as differing through the cultures of the world.[9]

Emotions become complex as feeling-arousing situations are compounded throughout life. More than one emotion is called forth in situations, i.e., grief may be compounded by shock, sadness, relief, anger, emptiness, and/or gladness. The richness of feelings, expressions and accumulation of experience add to the personality wealth of the aging person. In years of Summing Up, feelings are prime. Complexity of feelings are recognized and available for resolving life-long situations. Some examples, as forgiveness, acceptance, empathy, appreciation of rancor remain with us in quiet moments as we reconsider our life. Expressions have become more subtle, sometimes more guarded but infinitely more important in life. Feelings that ring joy, contentment, and peace guide our choices. Consider now, the intricacy of feelings as expressed in a few examples.

The maturation of emotion from the early beginnings of life changes in expression and depth. Let us take a brief look at possible end points of a few emotions and their effects on personality.

Forgiveness: Forgiveness involves many feelings beginning with hurt, insult, anger, misunderstandings, or rejection that may linger for years. An incident may alienate family or friend for years as the individual(s) retain feelings of unreconcilable experiences. The Biblical tale of the prodigal son who left home, "running away." He is welcomed warmly by his parents upon returning home, forgiven by his parents. Running away seems a common experience in our present culture with the adventuresome impulses of youth, or added dangers of drug addiction, abuse, etc. Forgiveness to the self and to another is a gift; a gift that enables warmth and love to emerge.

When Joan (aged 47) found that her daughter had been molested by her brother when the daughter was ten years old. Joan was enraged disappointed, even unbelieving. She told her brother - in anger, disbelief, disgust, hatred – to get out of her life. Joan never wanted to see him again, write him, or communicate with him anyway – ever. Now 74 years old, she had no contact with her brother for twenty years. Somehow the bitterness and hatred had melted. She longed for the intimacy, relationship and interactions that she had with him and his family. Joan recalled the closeness and the fun they had shared. She no longer hated him, wanted to see, forgive, and to love him again. Life was not worth the absence. At first, fearful of his reactions and rejection, telephone conversations renewed the contact.

What had happened to those complex feelings? Several forces had intervened. She could re-evaluate the incident, considering the many experiences gleaned during the years of separation. She could acknowledge that she could be partly responsible, she considered that pushing him away did not resolve the problem, that her anger and hostility had at first consumed her. With time, and many other emotional experiences, and with thought, the force of her feelings was lost. Her anger were dissolved; yes, she could "remember" but without the strong arousal that first occurred. Memories did not cloud her feelings. She could forgive him.

Most of all, we need to remember and forgive ourselves. Sadly, although a warm telephone conversation ensued, she died before a meeting could occur. Sometimes holding onto and nurturing feelings interfere with deeper longings and wishes.

Frank was an eighty-year-old veteran, hero of wars and of killing. Upon returning home from the armed services, he suffered severely from PTSD. He had killed other men, women, even children. Yet, he had to know he could kill, even though he had been a mild-mannered, soft-spoken person before the war. With psychotherapy, he came to accept that killing, destroying, being destructive was a part of himself, that he did not need to honor that part of himself by wrapping himself inside those actions. He learned to accept the destructive part of himself, to acknowledge it, not push it away. Only then, could his kindness, his care for others and his love for family emerge again. He could forgive himself. Emotional trauma can temporarily or permanently damage the personality. Even severe trauma can usually be lessened with introspection and help.

Rancor: Rancor embodies feelings of hate, bitterness, and continuing anger about an event of the past. Bitterness arises from continued disappointments and hurts in life. It presents the expectation of rejection, disappointment, failed relationships and grave injustices. It contains experience of righteous anger at remembered abusiveness, rumination over a sense of victimization, and anger that fester, growing into permanent expectations of smoldering resentments.[10] Often, of even most often, its beginnings flow from childhood, giving a dark coloring to experiences.

In the period of Summing Up, rancor takes a guise as a "stubborn old man," thereby giving social freedom to continue the negative expectations, critical attitudes, and interpersonal rejection. It is often enough a sad commentary on one's life. Yet, the sense of gratitude for life, contentment and pleasantness may eke out from the person. For underlying the rancor is the realization that living this long has entailed a share of the pleasant fruition of life.

Empathy: Empathy represents an epitome of emotions in relationships with others. It is a rare experience of intense interpersonal sensitivity. Empathy shows a deepness in relationships and a mature sensitivity to another; it involves a sharing, a oneness of feelings. Empathy is vicariously experiencing the feelings and actions of another. Empathy with another's sorrow brings the physical sense of another's sorrow. It represents a unity of feelings with another's distress and suffering, arousing compassion.

Less discussed, yet equally true, is the empathy with joyfulness of another. Sharing of joy and peacefulness also bring a forceful bonding with another.

Feelings that indicate an acknowledgement of another's emotional state include words as sympathy, compassion, pity, commiserations., etc. Pity acknowledges discomfort and distress of another, even at times commiserating that the state is undeserved or implying a sense of condescension. People are often disturbed when receiving "pity" from another. It is a reaction to the difficulties of the other, without help or resolution offered. Sympathy involves a feeling of care and concern for the other. It is a mirroring of the feelings and distress, often with the wish to help.

Guilt: Guilt may follow and besiege throughout life. Threading its way in feelings from childhood, it is based on fear, on losing esteem, or love from another. Guilt is an emotional reaction when one experiences inner turmoil at having done something – or failed to act - that he/she believes should not have done. Guilt provokes anxiety-ridden, ambivalent actions; it darkens decisions and actions; and it decreases confidence in the self. A life of guilt results in fear, suspiciousness, and anxiousness. With guilt-ridden persons, there is a need to please and reluctance to offer one' judgments, preferences, or wishes. It is "whatever you like," "you choose first."

Guilt interferes with psychological growth. It protects a person from rejection, yes, but more likely a guard against doing or saying something unacceptable. It darkens a sense of freedom, and, moreover, stifles curiosity. Guilt brings storms to life; possibly pacified by acknowledgement of action or thought. Accepting that "I did (or felt or thought) an untoward act is a step toward self-confidence.

Acceptance: One emotion tendered in life is an acceptance of one's own feelings, which precedes acceptance of another's' feelings. Awareness of one's feelings is a prerequisite for an honesty about oneself. Knowledge then demands knowing the situation that evoked feelings and actions. The assessment leads to understanding the reaction and evaluating the result. Self-examination will lead to accepting positive and negative aspects, whether quietly felt or openly expressed with actions and words.

Accepting oneself means to encounter inner feelings and memories honestly – whether pleasantness, loves, hatreds, stubbornness, angers that linger, hostile impulses that rankle, caring with sympathy, all. When we can accept our self, honestly and forthrightly, the inner storms of life are subdued. Then we can accept others as they are – without criticism, or fault finding, or withdrawal. Honesty with oneself precedes acceptance of others. This is not tolerance – for tolerance signifies "to put up with." Acceptance is an emotional openness – to situations, to others – to life. Acceptance calms the waters.

I have a vivid memory of an unfortunate childhood incident. There were seven children in our family. If was the fifth child, with a younger sister and brother. For dinner we all sat around an oval table with mother and father at each end. Once, when I was about five years old, my oldest sister was serving a bowl of soup to my two-year-old brother, who sat next to me. My elbow jerked upwards, and she spilled the hot soup on his leg, burning him. She jumped, alarmed, crying and apologetic. I remember being scared and shocked. I felt I had been bad; Did I do it on purpose? It was an impulse, not a thought or feeling. An aside comment here, impulses are pure actions, without a feeling imposed.

I have lived with this memory. I had been a bad girl, done a mean thing. Had I really caused an accident that hurt my sister and little brother? This is not a favorite memory. It has served me well, however, for I learned early that I could be bad. This incident sensitized me. I became the "good girl" in the family. I had discovered that actions could cause physical and psychological hurt to others. To know oneself is to realize the depth of good and bad impulses, actions and feelings that are contained within oneself.

Acceptance is being open to the actual feelings of the moment by moment and being willing to feel whatever they are. Whether there is: anger, happiness, fear, jealousy, anxiety, joy. We can learn to simply BE with our experience.

Acceptance of others is based on knowledge of and acceptance of oneself. An acquiescence of all.

SUMMARY

Feelings come and go endlessly, as the waves of the ocean. Sometimes feelings are quiet, like peaceful waves that gently wash the sands of the shores. In the Summing Up and Encore periods, quiet times are often filled with contentment and peace, and a quiet joy for life. Other times, the wave in life are rampant uncontrollable, even washing away some of the sands lining the shore. Emotional stresses leave us footless, eroding basic principles of being. Emotions sometimes overwhelm the path of life, and leave us stranded, without clear choice or action. Yes, learning control and expression of emotions has been a challenging task. Control has enabled a fruitful use of the heights and depths of life's challenges. Control often worked to our advantage; yet too much control squelches the feelings and the character.

Experience has given knowledge of -

- When and how to use forgiveness for oneself and to grant it to another. Forgiveness of the self yields self-knowledge and personal enrichment. Forgiveness for another is a gift that yields the possibility of acceptance and love to emerge.
- When and how to forgive the trespass. Forgiveness for oneself brings welcome warmth to the water; forgiveness for others brings a smooth pathway to a relationship
- When and how to accept the unsure, anxious stirrings within. Quietness, and contemplation provide a wealth of inner support; acceptance calms uncertain waters.
- When and how to have empathy. Empathy comes from within us. It is the opening of one's feelings to another's. A sharing of oneness - often unexpected, overwhelming, awesome.
- When and how to know acceptance. For the self, it quiets unwanted inner storms of self-doubt and lets it be. Acceptance of others permit an invitation to another's world and opens our world to everyone. It is acquiescence.
- When love enters, it brings warmness to life. We feel it, know it. Love has ever been acknowledged as the ultimate emotion.

Positivity colors these last periods of life. A positive, pleasant attitude persists, despite storms. The storms may be recognized as worse than before, probably because it is uncontrollable, unexpected, and dangerous. Even so, positivity reigns.

The next chapters deal with some of these stresses – a positive attitude persists and will soothe the waters.

REFERENCES

1. Albert H. Hastorf (1997) Lewis Terman's Longitudinal Study of the Intellectually Gifted: Early Research, Recent Investigations and the Future, Gifted and Talented International, 12:1,3-7, DO I:10,1080/15332276,1997,1167288

2. Friedman, Howard W. Tucker, Joan S., Tomlinson-Keasey, Carol, Schwartz, Joseph E., Wingard, Deborah I., and Criqui, Michael H; 1993. "Does Childhood Personality Predict Longevity?" Journal Personality and Social Psychology. Vol. 65, No. 1 176-185.

3. May, Ulrich, Editor. 2016. Authors, Mathew A. Harris, Caroline E. Brett, Wendy Johnson, and Ian J. Deary)" Personality Stability from Age 14 to Age 77 years." Psychol Aging 2016 De. 31(8) 862-874). Also, the extensive research by Laura Carstensen et al at Stanford University i.e., Charles, Susan and Carstensen, Laura discuss the reasons for this positivity shift in an article, Social and Emotional Aging, 2014. Annu Rev Psychol. 2010, 61:383-409) Further, A meta-analysis published in 2014 based on 100 studies concluded that the positivity effect is reliable (Reed, Andrew E., Chan, Larry and Mikels, Joseph A. A. in "Meta-Analysis of the Age-Related Positivity Effect: Age Differences in Preferences for Positive Over Negative Information. In Psychology and Aging, 2014, Vol. 29, No. 1, 1-15.

4. Reed, Andrew and Carstensen, Laura L "The theory behind the Age-Related Positivity Affect www.ncbi.nim.nit.gov. Front. Psychol. 2012. Sept 2.doi

5. As reported in "The Theory Behind the Age-Related Positivity Effect" www.nbi.nim.nih.gov

6. Plutchiik, Robert (1991) The Basic Emotions, Revised Edition. New York: Barnes and Noble.

7. Blanchard and Fields, 2007 Blanchard-Fields F. Everyday problem solving and emotion: an adult developmental perspective. Curr. Dir. Psychol. Sci. 16 1 26-31 10.1111/j.1467-8721.2007.00469.x - DOI)

8. Plutchik, Robert (1991) The Basic Emotions, Revised Edition.

New York: Barnes and Noble.

9. https.//psychologyy-spot.com/list of-emotions-and-and feelings/ Last updated 04/02/2020.

10. Leon F. Seltzer, Ph, D, 2015. "Don't let your Anger "Mature" into Bitterness." https://www.psychologytoday.com/us/evolution-the-self/201501/don't-let-your-anger-mature-bitterness.

CHAPTER FIVE

Alone Lonely Isolation Depression

The waves roll in...endlessly...rolling... one wave remains...it does not fit the rhythm of other waves...it is alone...yet caught by a huge wave that rolls over and over... not flowing with the waves... alone in the ocean...

ALONE

The depth of aloneness fills the spirit. At times, to be alone is sought, is yearned for. Alone. I well remember times when I longed for a week alone...a week to spend deep in the forest, among trees, with songs of birds, to eradicate the distance from myself, to replenish an inner void. Peace.

Then a thought fills awareness – I am alone, alone to live, alone to die. All the people around me are alone – what is this sense? This feeling?

Aloneness is not a feeling. It is consciousness of the self. Diverse, disparate feelings may accompany aloneness. It may bring physical relief, delight of the spirit, gladness of the soul, an emotional high; it may bring a deep awareness of life, a sadness of loss, an eradication of others, even anger. Time alone is often welcome - time to take care for one's self, to manage those personal matters, to think, even to do those little things that beg for attention.

Many elderly persons face alone-ness, and especially with the loss of a partner, a spouse. In past years, an adult child would assume responsibility for their parents and home. Families in the last century could not imagine the tremendous alone-ness that elderly persons now suffer. The role of adult children with parents is not clearly defined in our culture. In the present situation, parents want to retain independence, do not wish to rely upon the assistance from children and find themselves alone. Yet, even unconsciously, parents desire to retain intimacy with and receive care from children. Aloneness with aging is difficult.

In 2010, thirteen percent of Americans were over 65 years of age; by 2030, the number will jump to twenty percent. In 1900, only one hundred thousand Americans lived to be 85 years or more; by 2010, those one hundred thousand persons living beyond 85 years will be five and one-half million, not counting those living in nursing homes or hospitals. Presently, over eleven million elderly persons live alone.[1]

Thirty-seven percent of elderly women and nineteen percent of elderly men live alone. About seventy-two percent of older men live with a spouse; only forty-two percent of older women still have a partner. Considering the inequality of racial or ethnic persons, non-Hispanic and black women are more likely than women of other races to live alone – thirty-nine percent; only twenty-one percent of older Asian women and twenty-three percent of older Hispanic women live alone. These figures represent cultural differences as well as economic problems. The trend is that the likelihood of living alone increases with age. For women over 75 years, almost half are living alone.

ALONE THEN LONELINESS

How to capture aloneness? When does it first become known or experienced? Is it in the fears of darkness of the child who huddles under blankets fearful of each creak? Is it in the sense of the child left alone at Summer Camp for the first time? Is it in the utter sadness with an adolescent excluded from a teenage party? It seems already evident when a crying infant is comforted simply by being held in someone's arms. Feeling alone in old age is to suffer deeply.

Aloneness unwanted brings loneliness. It can bring fear, with no one present to help in case of need. No one is there for love or intimacy. It can surfeit the emptiness around one, the space, the unfillable space with no one there. Fears are embedded within loneliness. Many, even most, elderly persons, face the last years of life alone, in illness and dying. Aloneness is ever there.

The awareness of the fragility of being elderly and alone gradually sets upon the person, often accelerated by disability or illness. My aunt, physically healthy and living in an independent residential community for seniors, was at a loss when she could no longer drive her Saab for errands and shopping. She was alone. No one there to care for her. And now, she felt trapped. Encouraged to call a taxi, she could not face the possible danger of being alone with an unknown person. She felt frightened and unable to take care for herself.

Loneliness settles upon the spirit of the elderly meeting its fullness with the loss of a life's partner. What happens now? Can I travel alone? Can I go shopping alone? Can I even take a long drive into the country alone? Faced with the reality, loneliness creeps in – the need for a sense of closeness with others, that someone really cares. The family – children and grandchildren – become primary sources of comfort. Even with the family, the space is filled only occasionally. They have their own lives, their own responsibilities, their own friends." I don't want to be a burden on the children" – "I don't expect them to take care of me," "They have their own lives." These are common responses of parents, comforting themselves, and pushing aside their wish for more support from adult children. Yet, the longing to fill the aloneness is there. She could not tell her two adult daughters that she was lonely, that she needed their company a bit more. Often children have not anticipated nor have been physically or emotionally prepared or ready to assume responsibility for caring for aging parents.

Aloneness becomes loneliness, especially when being alone is not desired or enjoyed. Earlier in life, loneliness differs from aloneness. In younger days, loneliness may be the longing for a lover, a special friend or home. In age, it tends to be the longing for what once was, the homestead, familiar places, old friends. Aloneness does not bring the woes of loneliness, loneliness brings longing for the presence of a special person – a sibling, parent, a child, an old friend, the neighborhood one left behind. It may be a feeling of missing the person, the desire to share, to talk, to be with the person. "Oh, I would enjoy telling M...this story, she would love it."

The extreme of loneliness is deeper yet; not only is there a sense of lostness, but isolation may take over. The rhythm of life is gone. This kind of aloneness is not desired. Isolation feels like a desert, nothing on the sands that give meaning. Time is longer, days are darker, meaningless...away from people. Isolation is the sense of utter aloneness covered by sadness, longing, nostalgia. Fears of aloneness, feelings of being abandoned, an absence of feeling warm and loved. Loneliness wraps itself in a blanket, huddles alone in the search for warmth, wanting, wanting, no one to love, no one to really care.

Mary, 85 years of age, has an apartment in a senior citizen community. A frail, thin lady, she moved to the community after her husband of forty years had died. There were no children. Moving from a large home to a one-bedroom apartment was frightening and traumatic. In the community, she would come to meals early, carrying a book with paper to write upon. Fearful of others, she would sit alone at a table, her head lowered, and peeking through her glasses at other tables full of people. She was very alone. When invited to sit with others with bowed head, she would refuse the overture from others. She ate quickly and returned to her room. Isolated. Then isolating herself further in her apartment, her fear of others was quieted; she sobs in loneliness.

Aging brings many changes that impact loneliness and evoke isolation as an easier path. In one study, participants were asked to describe a situation in which they felt loneliness. Over forty loneliness feelings were described. Among these were: self-pity (32%), a feeling that no one understood them (17%), helplessness (24%), a sense of being different (20%), boredom (14%), and rejected by others (18%). [2]

In the United States about twenty-seven percent of persons aged sixty and older live alone. In many countries, fewer than five percent of older persons live alone – this even includes countries in the Asia-Pacific area, Saharan Africa, and the Middle East-North African regions as well as Afghanistan, Mali and Algeria. [3]

My heart is deeply scarred, burned as I look around and think of the elderly persons, alone and so deeply lonely. Time is endless. Days have little purpose. No plans for the day, just a day to be. When illness or disability complicates living – and it will, because eighty-five percent of seniors of eighty years suffer from at least two chronic illnesses. Further complications are often present with difficulties in hearing, seeing, walking, balance, or other physical movements. [4] The search for escape from loneliness and isolation, the search for meaning, becomes depressing.

As a psychologist, I have been led to an understanding of the role of schedules in the daily life of people and especially of the function, utility, and comfort, and necessity of compulsive activities in life.

A long time ago, I was seeing an eight-year-old boy in psychotherapy. He would come into the room, look around for something to do, and inevitably pick up a bean bag and throw it in the basket, counting each throw – -up to hundreds, not stopping. Trying to understand the meaning of the game, I asked him how it felt. He replied he did not have to feel if he were playing. Then he said he could tell me how it felt - if he could climb on a shelf and be above me. Which he did, and his feelings came tumbling out of his mouth.

What did this tell me? In the time that the elderly spends alone, much time is given to activities that provides for relaxation and comforting of feelings. The activities demand repetition – playing games, crocheting, painting, doing crossword puzzles or sudoku puzzles, etc. The activities bring enjoyment, purpose, and relaxation. Such activities are to be honored, many of them bringing out a creativity that has lain dormant and unused throughout a lifetime. Other activity provide learning of new techniques or ideas. These are means of expressing and honoring ungratified feelings lying deeply within.

In the Summing Up period, the elderly often speak of their life as having no purpose. There is little purpose for them that is recognized by others or by society as important. Certainly, loneliness is increased when comparisons are made to others, especially to younger years or peoples. Now it is important to focus on one's self, to claim life and the right to enjoy living.

Mary is eighty-five years old, wears glasses, has some hearing problems, and conquered breast cancer. She lives in an apartment within a senior citizen complex. She wanted to maintain her independence, to control her life, and to manage those mundane tasks necessary for living. She decided to assign a different task to each day. For instance, she assigned Sunday for going to church; Mondays were for washing clothes; Tuesdays had the task of shopping at the local grocery; Wednesday is telephoning and talking with her son, who resides in another state; Thursday and Saturday are days of playing bridge with others in the complex; Friday is meal planning for the week and house-attention day; and Saturdays are open, unplanned. This plan kept her busily occupied and engaged with living.

One of the more pleasant times occurs when adult children include visiting or being with the parent on a regular schedule. This gives the parent a sense of control over her/his days and a security in the relationship. The visit is "something to look forward to."

LONELINESS TO ISOLATION

Loneliness looms hugely over days. As it takes over, a pulling away from people may take place, the aged person becomes isolated. Relatives and friends die. Whether it is the strangeness of a new environment, as in a community of senior citizens, or in a setting as a rehabilitation center when some help with life's tasks becomes necessary, or as in assisted living communities, or in settings for memory problems, isolation threatens. Or even, when living alone in one's house for years, loneliness results in pulling away from friends, relatives, or once-beloved activities – isolation.

Huge loneliness, that monster, looms ahead for many aged persons. The sense of freedom gets crushed with emptiness. Overwhelming loneliness and isolation eradicate sense of freedom to do what one wants, especially with age setting upon one.

Isolation sets in – isolation from family, friends, social groups, as church groups. By age seventy-five, half of women in our country live alone. The challenge is there... alone, isolated..., now what? For many plans had been made, so there are things to do. Yet, inner sense of loneliness often pervades.

Amy, a retired professor now ninety years old, lived alone after her husband of fifteen years, died. Once a busy teacher, she had gradually lost contact with friends. She became more and more isolated from the world outside her home. Caring for her husband had consumed her time. Now alone, isolated, no family or friends remaining, her health declined severely. Gradually, she had closed more rooms in her house; lights were used only in her bedroom. She lay in bed all days and nights, gradually losing physical strength, and able only to crawl to the bathroom.

I tried talking with her of possibilities - at-home caretaker, live-in nurse, assisted living homes, social workers, counselors – she would have none. I tried a report to social services, although she did not wish it. A social worker visited. Amy accepted no help whatsoever. Totally isolated, except for unannounced visits, she lay almost motionless, occasionally reading the financial news that came regularly. Visiting her one morning, she had died alone during the night.

Loneliness and isolation are an epidemic among senior citizens. The statistics are awesome. The lack of social connections is as detrimental to health as smoking fifteen cigarettes a day; coronary bypass patients who report feeling lonely have a mortality rate five times higher than other patients thirty days post-surgery; lonely persons have a sixty-four percent increased chance of developing clinical dementia; and lonely persons report five percent more severe symptoms of the common cold than those who are less lonely.[5]

ISOLATION TO DEPRESSION

Depression is like a whirlpool, pulling one further and further down into nothinglessness. It is: A deep, dark hole that forces questions of the value of living: A dark endless vortex. The person is lost and contact with others is almost nil.

Isolation gives way to depression. When a person is not in contact with others who have personal significance, the isolated person gradually accommodates to the lack of people in his or her life. Submitting to the aloneness, the loneliness, and the isolation brings a deprivation of health-given activity and of socialization so necessary for well-being. The habituation to isolation is a pathway to depression.

Depression seldom overtakes one suddenly; a gradual onset of symptoms may come. And the interference of normal reactions or activities may not be immediately observable to others. Three core symptoms are: low mood, anhedonia, and a reduction of energy.

A low mood, like being "down in the dumps," is a normal experience. When difficult events or experiences come, such as relationship problems, bereavement. Illness, or sleep problems are common. A general low mood includes sadness, worry, tiredness, frustration, or anger. Generally, a low mood will tend to lift after a few days. It is when the low mood persists for two weeks, and when there is no obvious reason for the mood, that it may be a sign of depression.

Anhedonia reflects difficulty in finding pleasure in activities or with people. Disgruntled with everything, it is a loss of ability to feel joy, food does not taste good, comfort or hugs from others is not welcome. The third symptom of depression refers to reduced energy levels and increased tiredness. Often depression is an avoidance of life through sleep, which brings the loss of energy or desire for moving about. It may be expressed through self-neglect, feelings of guilt, low interest level, anxiety, impaired ability to concentrate, sleep disturbance, some irritability or agitation, and suicidal thoughts.

Depression in the elderly is a pervasive problem. Not only may it be caused by physical illnesses or disabilities, but it may also increase the severity of any illness. Depression may be confused in work with older adults for physical illnesses and disabilities are more easily recognized as the problem. Sometimes a depressed person may be misunderstood and the person accused of simply wanting to avoid life' tasks.

"II the person has to do" – in the eyes of the other – "is to behave normally."

The onset of depression in the elderly is recognized as having several causal factors, or a combination of them, that contribute to depression. First is a family history of depression: in these instances, persons with a family history of depression are more likely to develop depression in aging. One person I knew, a well-esteemed and vivacious college professor, had been "fighting" depression most of her life. She traced her family history and discovered that over forty relatives had suffered serious depressive episodes in the course of their lives. She, herself, had several episodes of depression. This awareness of the family history relieved her of the guilt she had long carried. She had assumed she was doing something wrong in her living. With this information, she was able to ward off the onset of depression helped by appropriate medications. Sad to observe, her colleagues saw the episodes as a kind of escapism from work. There seems to be a genetic factor that may predispose toward depression, which has not been specifically identified.

For the elderly who experience depression for the first time, the depression may be related to changes in the brain and body, brought about by aging or illness. Often, an illness, or the medications given for the illness, may have an effect that contributes to depressive symptoms. This is especially so with serious medical illnesses as diabetes, cancer, heart disease and Parkinson's disease.[6]

Another related cause for geriatric depression is found in the life histories of those who have been maltreated or abused as children. The impact of childhood trauma that involved physical, sexual, and emotional abuse leads toward increased onsets of depression in older years. In one study, 8,051 adults, aged over sixty year were given questions that addressed physical and sexual abuse in childhood. Six different types of questions from the Adult Childhood Experiences were asked, such as: parents being physically abusive to each other, the child being physically harmed by a parent, being sworn at by the parent, being touched sexually by an adult, being forced to sexually touch an adult, and being forced into intercourse. The types of abuse, especially repeated physical abuse, and repeated sexual intercourse, were significantly related to depression in older ages.[7]

Other studies have shown the importance of childhood relationships with parents and the effect on the child throughout life. In another study involving nearly three thousand adults, the adults were asked their recollections of parents during childhood. Questions as – How much could you confide in her or him about things that were bothering you?" "How much did he or she understand your problems and worries?" "How much love or affection did she or he give you?" The adults were then asked to respond to questions that rated different feelings of depressive symptoms as how often they felt: sad, nervous, hopeless, worthless. A significant relationship was shown between those reporting lack of parental support during childhood and increased levels of depressive symptoms and chronic health conditions problems persisting throughout adulthood into old age.[8] The sadness of childhood was uncovered and re-emerged in aging.

Depression is an illness. It is not an act of will of a person as was sometimes thought. It is not an illness brought on by lethargy or loss of will. Stressful events accompanied by social isolation may have such an impact that it triggers a depression. Grief over loss of family or friends may increase social withdrawal and eventuate in a depression. To the contrary, evidence has been shown that older adults who have strong social ties and a sense of community are less likely to experience depression and remain healthier also.[9]

Treatment for depression begins with seeking professional help. This may be a medical doctor, psychologist, psychiatrist, or another mental-health professional. If the symptoms indicate a depression, a choice for treatment may include psychotherapy, medication, or both. Other alternative treatments include physical exercise which has been shown to have an effect that increases positive moods and alleviates some heaviness of depression.

If the depression is severe and/or chronic, there are additional treatments that have proven effective. The treatment may involve electrical stimulation of the neurons in the brain. It is necessary to consult a specialist in the two or three different approaches that may be considered with the doctor.

RELIEF FROM ALONENESS;
HELP FOR ISOLATION

These days are the summation of life. To be among the oldest-old is awesome. Many family and friends have long gone. You are at a loss, not knowing what to do. How then can we live these days with a spirit of thankfulness, a spirit of fulfilled goals and dreams. The loneliness and isolation creeps into the soul. Loneliness and depression are rooted in feelings of the absence or loss of love that often pervades in the elderly. The following brief notes may help you guide your own way through the days.

We are in the Summing Up and Encore Phases. We have experienced a gradual loss of the physical freedom granted youth. Freedom now arises from within. To retain this inner freedom relies upon conscious effort. Yes, it was easier before; now the simple life necessities take thought and effort.

The following comments are gauged to help retain that inner sense of freedom and of the self. These are offered as simple principles to help in greeting, meeting, and enjoying life.

1. **This is life.** It is yours only. Yours to enjoy, or not, as you choose. Yours to live each day. Choose how you want to meet each day: with a smile, even in pain; with curiosity of what the day may bring; with something new to do or learn.

2. **Spend time outdoors.** Impel yourself to engage in being out-of-doors at least one-half hour each day. Breathe the air, enjoy the weather, consciously observe the natural surroundings, the natural life around.

3. **Make a plan.** To be in control of your life involves a sense that you are aware of what you will do, which makes for a sense of security and predictability about the nest day. Each evening make a plan for yourself.

Write it down. Include little things as: Morning activities, lunch, afternoon time, dinner time and evenings.

Before retiring at night, review the next day's activities. In the morning, look at it. Have an outlined plan appropriate for most days include details as: what shall I have for breakfast If you can, make the plan for each day for the week.

4. **Contact with others.** Make certain that you contact at least one person every day – in face-to-face time, or on the telephone, or sending a card. Add a social interaction for each day, even if talking to the clerk in a store, add a social meeting, zoom program, even watch how others move about. Impel a personal contact with another.

5. **Find something new each day.** Look about you, discover something new – in observations, in reading, in a hobby, in a ae, a topic or unexplored interest. Many find an impetus for new activity and interest during their fifties; others have kept

*How to fill in all those empty hours.

If you are fortunate to have a hobby or activity that you love, now is the opportunity for them, there are: 1. Activities for the hands, as art or craft, musical talents to increase or develop, sewing crafts, woodworking skills; 2. Activities for the mind, as crossword puzzles, sudoku puzzles, reading; 3. Activities for leisure as listening to music, watching television programs; 4. Activities for social interactions as bridge, other card games, puzzles to solve.

The process of growing old and older yet passes through several stages. The acceptance of being elderly brings a redefinition of the self. At the age of ninety-two, I have not yet told myself that "I am a really old person." "I am elderly". My age tells me differently. Elderly is not part of my self-concept...yet I am certainly within that age description. Aloneness and increasing isolation from third and fourth generation of my primary family roots and from long known friends are here. Isolation will be increased when this writing is finished. Isolation. Aloneness. This is what all elderly people encounter. However graciously or angrily the aloneness is met is yet to be seen. This is my life. This is your life. To live it as fully as possible, to enjoy each minute and day, to share our spirits with others. That is enough.

REFERENCES

1. The sources of this data come from the 2017 Profile of Older Americans, the U.S. Census Bureau and the National Center for Health Statistics, U.S. Department of Health and Human Services

2. Loneliness. Reported by: www.psychologyandsociety.con/loneliness.htl

3. Ausibe;. Jacob. "Fact Tank-News in the Number." "Older people are more likely to live alone in the U.S. than elsewhere in the World." March 10, 2020 http://wwwpewresearch.org/fac/tank/2020/03older-olderpeople-are-more-likely-to-live-alone-in-the-U-S-than-elsewhere-in-the-world/

4. Administration on Aging. 2018, "2017 Profile of Older Americans" U.S. Department of Health and Human Services.

5. These statistics are reported in http://www.stonegtes;wpengine.com/ 19. From the National Institute on Aging

6. "Depression and Older Adult". 8/4/20. An article from the National Institute on Aging. https://www.nia.nih.gov/health/depression-and-older adults.

7. Margaret A. Eggs, Erick Messias Puru Thapa, and Lewis P. Krain 2010. "Adverse Childhood Experiences and Geriatric Depressio: Results fro the 2010 BRFSS. Am.J.Geriatr Psychiatry. https://www.ncbi/nim.nih.gov/prm/article/PMC4267899/

8. Benjamin A. Shaw, et al., 2004. "Emotional Support fro Parents Early in Life, Aging and Health" in Psychology and Aging, 2001, Vol. 19, No 1, 4-12.

9. Naprawa, Amanda. 2020. "Spotting Depression in Older Adults" http://www.berkeleywellness.com/health-mind/mood/article/sppootting-depression-in-older-adult.

CHAPTER SIX

Confidence And Trust Lost
Life In A Hurtful World

For a while, the waters flow smoothly...Yet here comes a side rush of river, crashing... the water's course forcefully changed... and yet, stronger, and more dangerous ...onward, onward, onward... each side stream increasing force, altering the flow even more...and ...changing the flow... invading and disturbing...the waters bend and recoil ...never to regain?

INTRODUCTION

This chapter discusses the hurtful side of human relations often endured by elders. The course of life has embraced the warmth, the goodness, the joys of sacrifice in life, and the bonds of love shared with partners, children, friends, and others. Many an elder person now faces a growing need for reciprocity of care given as the weakness of illness, the aching of body, the failing strength to care for oneself impertinently interferes with fulfillment of life. Weakness and disability have usurped the strength for self-care, for self-expression, for self-protection. And now, subjected for care/attention from others, all too many must endure inappropriate actions, or pent-up anger, or misdirected hostility/hatred.

Social interactions are affected by feelings toward the other, his/her age, former relationship quality with them, intensity of relationship, social status, mood of the day, and mutual expectations. There are spoken and unspoken behaviors, conscious and unconscious reactions to others. Each person influences us, whether the occasion is spontaneous, unplanned, or expected, and despite our age.

Parents and siblings, children, friends, colleagues all bring a sense of ourselves with another. For instance, to one niece, I am a caring mother, to another an idolized aunt, to a friend, a confidant. There are bonds of warmth and love, of trust and confidence that enrich each day. With others, the elders have met with fear, withdrawal, coldness and distrust, avoidance, and hostility. None of these social encounters prepare for the neglect, physical abuse, and emotional trauma yet to come.

In this chapter we shall look at hurtful attitudes, behaviors and feelings directed toward elder persons, and how these interactions affect the elder person. It could be expected that there would be an increasing regard for our elders – our parents and grandparents – and a cultural morality that would reflect respect. That does not appear to be the case. There are forms of relating that deny respect, are hurtful, and are damaging to elders. These will be viewed on a continuum of intensity, from patronization to receiving unneeded or unwanted help, to social discrimination, to ostracization, microaggression, to neglect and abuse.

THE INCREASE OF ABUSE AND NEGLECT

Much has been written about the frequency of neglect and abuse of older persons in institutions as well as in their homes. A revealing study, published in 2015, explored negativity and/or positivity words describing the aged as presented in publications from 1810 to the present.[1] From 400 million words, thirteen thousand, one hundred words were rated for positive or negative attitudes. The conclusion: "We found that age stereotypes have become more negative in a linear way over 200 years. In 1880, age stereotype switched from being positive to being negative... The potential reasons were interpreted as related to a growing population and medicalization for the aging. Stereotypes were positive from 1810 to 1879, neutral words in 1880 and then switched to being negative. Negative attitudes toward elders have become increasingly negative during the following decades." It appears that negativity of attitudes toward the aged continues to increase into the twenty-first century.

Another indication of the present negative view of the elderly is described by Becca Levy. She looked at Facebook pages focusing on old age. She found extremely negative views of older people that went so far as to suggest killing off those over 69 years in a firing squad.[2] There is no decrease in our present age, despite legal attempts to control discrimination, infantilization and denigration.

MICROAGGRESSION TOWARD ELDERLY

Negative attitudes run in a continuum from stereotypes that characterize the elderly in everyday speech, to semi-conscious words that are used to address the elderly, to forms of aggressive allusions, harassment, and isolation. These expressions of "everyday exchanges that send denigrating messages to certain individuals because of their group membership" are called *microaggression* by psychologist Derald Wing Sue. They are terms that describe "brief and common place daily verbal, behavioral and environmental indignities, whether intentional or unintentional that communicate hostile, derogatory or negative slights and insults to the target person or group."

Addressing an elderly lady, the restaurant waiter says: "May I help you, young lady?" The elderly lady may have a slight surge of pleasure when called "young lady" yet, she knows and feels it as a denial of her actual person. Other examples: "You don't look that old," "old geezer," "grumpy old man." Or when a doctor questions the daughter, who has accompanied her mother, rather than talk to the mother, asks the daughter, "Does she take her medicine regularly?" While mother is sitting there, ignored, as if she could not understand the questions, and treated like a child. These microaggressive comments may be overlooked by the older person even though being disrespected and ignored.

I have a beloved niece who is charming and helps – even

though and when, I do not want or need it. "Oh, let me do it" (carry a cup of coffee to the table); Or surprised at an activity, "I did not think you could do this" (work at a picture puzzle). I love her attention but am a tiny bit irritated at trying to understand what made her think I might have trouble with placing pieces in a puzzle- I do recognize that she moves more quickly than I!

As this intentional or unintentional aggressive behavior becomes more active, it becomes teasing, then *harassment.* "Get out of my way, old man" "you are too old to try that?" Harassment involves intentional aggressive comments or behaviors, shown in repeated or prolonged offensive words or actions. It is commonly understood as behavior that demeans, humiliates, or embarrasses a person, and these are behaviors that are disturbing, upsetting or threatening to the person. "That dress is out of style."

The elderly person may be deeply offended by these "little" aggressive comments, inured to the insults, or to the person who often teases. "No more golf for you, old man," Or, "You are a cripple", "you talk funny." The elderly person may simply walk away, try to ignore the message, sometimes question the other's intent, apologize for a comment by the aggressor, or sometimes just becomes bewildered and hurt.

Discrimination is another type of silent aggression; discrimination is a quiet isolation of the elder. Conversation within a group discussion may quietly exclude responses or feelings of a present elder. Example: my mother was an active member of a women's church group for over twenty years. Good friends, all, in the group. However, the group grew younger with new members and a new, younger leader.

Then came the day when mother was told to prepare the yarn, rather than participate in the patterning of a quilt – isolating her from the specific work she had created, from friends she knew so well, and placing her with a younger, less familiar group of people. Whatever the reasons I cannot know; I am only aware of the deep hurt, even insult, that mother expressed as she was isolated from friends. Isolation becomes more common as a person ages.

NEGLECT AND ABUSE

Alice (age 72) found herself in a rehab-assisted living hospital following surgery for a knee replacement. She had chosen a place highly rated for the care and accommodations offered. The second afternoon, she needed help to get to the bathroom; ringing the bell and waiting over one-half hour, she attempted to walk the short distance alone, slipped and fell. Hurt from falling and loss of control, she lay for a while on the floor, then tried to return to the bed. The humiliation of losing bowel control was horrid enough but crawling back into bed on the floor was worse. Severe neglect.

It is estimated that over four million elderly Americans are subjected to physical, psychological, and other forms of abuse and neglect each year whether in a caring institution or at home. That includes at least one in ten elderly persons, but many abuses are not reported because the elderly person is unwilling, ashamed, or unable to tell someone. For each case of neglect and abuse that is reported, experts estimate as many twenty-three cases are not reported. Further, persons eighty years and older suffer abuse and neglect two to three times more frequently. Obviously, as one becomes older, more feeble, or weak, disabled, ill, more abuse can be expected. While hospitals or care institutions must report neglect and abuse, most abusers are family members, most often an adult child or caretaker; the frequency cannot be estimated because the abuse is not reported unless the person is taken for medical care.[3]

> Jane (age 88), lived with her daughter, Susan, and her husband. Jane had invited them to live with her because of her need for physical help. Susan and her husband chose to live with Jane. In recompense, they were to have mother's house, upon her death. Jane had Parkinson's disease, giving her difficulty in walking, and some memory problems. One day Susan, overwhelmed with her own anxieties, could not tolerate her mother's repeated questions about a dental appointment. In anger, Susan struck her mother's face, yelling, "don't ask me anymore."

Typical physical abuse includes hitting, pushing, slapping, beating, and spankings. Also restraining a person against his/her will, such as locking them in a room, tying them to a bed or furniture, or sexual abuse, whether forcing them passively to watch or participate in sexual acts.

John, aged 87, had suffered severe injury to his back and was bedfast. The caretaker settled him in a chair while making his bed. Suddenly, the caretaker left. John was alone, sitting in a chair. It was two hours before the caretaker returned. While the caretaker was gone, John suffered severe pain, had no means to signal for help, endured back pain, had screamed for help, and then passed out. His caretaker returned, not even apologetic. This is both neglect and abuse.

Neglect is abuse. While it is passive, it is the failure of a caregiver to meet the needs of a dependent, elderly person. Neglect may be intentional as in withholding of food, failure to provide medications, failure to clean or bathe the person, leaving the person isolated simply ignoring a need. Neglect includes physical, emotional social needs left unfulfilled, or withholding food, medications, or access for health care. It may be unintentional, as a result of genuine ignorance of results of the inattention or physical inability to address a particular need of the person.

A recent report of the New York Times described the careless approach of many nursing homes both in physical care and in medical responsiveness.[4] They report that half of nursing homes underreport ulcers (bed sores) by at least 50 per cent; about 40 percent fail to report injuries from serious falls, and that at least 1,200 nursing homes were cited for at least one incident related to possible abuse or neglect. The journalists report that rape was classified as "a low-level problem that causes "potential but not actual harm" to the patient. Yet rape is a criminal offense! Evidently, this is not so when acted against helpless, bedfast persons, or with elderly persons. Rape causes severe harm to the person. Damaging her/his sense of safety, of self-control, a sense of violation, shame, and humiliation to the person.

Consider briefly the following abusive situations:

John, aged 87, slightly demented, was locked in his bedroom because he once wondered alone from home to the local grocery store. He was permitted out of the room only when a male relative was present to control his actions.

Helen, aged ninety, would wander into other's rooms in the assisted living institution, occasionally falling asleep in a strange bed, or changing into that person's clothing. She was tied to her bed to keep her stationary and given "tranquilizing" medications.

Stephen constantly suffered severe abdominal pain after his wife's death. The doctors found no obvious cause. It was ruled as a sign of depression, and he was administered anti-depression and antipsychotic medication. After his death, it was discovered that his pain was real – a cancerous growth in his bowels. He was not hallucinating!

It is estimated that over five million elders over 65 have experienced some dementia. Of those over 85, about one-half have some form of Alzheimer's or other dementia. One study, completed in 2010, found that forty-seven per cent of those with dementia had been mistreated by caregivers.

About eight per cent had been abused psychologically, about twenty per cent had experienced some physical abuse, and about thirty per cent had experienced neglect as bed sores, lack of medications, hunger, etc.[5]

FINANCIAL ABUSE

Another form of abuse is becoming more frequent and difficult to detect. Financial abuse occurs when monies or possessions are stolen from an older person. Financial abuse is the illegal, unauthorized use of an elder's money, benefits, belongings or property, or assets for the benefit of someone other than the elder adult. It is becoming a wide-spread, personally intrusive issue most often by family members or caretakers. Increasingly, professional thieves invade the person's private life through the telephone, internet, or email all of which provides an opening into much private information, even financial monies.

Financial neglect may occur when the elder becomes unable to take care of financial responsibilities, such as paying the rent or other bills and they are ignored by a caretaker. Often, there may be financial exploitation in which the older's properties or assets are taken over and used by an adult child, relative or other person without consent of the person, even under false pretense or through intimidation. It is misuse of the elder's property or assets, using the assets without consent.

Often enough, an elder realizes some discomfort in managing his/her affairs, or a relative may sense the elder needs some help. He/she may take charge of an elder's monies and/or investments, sometimes obtaining control through the legal system.

Mary's (age 78) husband had died a couple months earlier. She had three adult daughters, (Jane, age 64), June (age 56) and Jill (age 54). After Mary's husband died, Mary complained to Jane that she was not certain that she was handling the financial matters correctly. Jane offered to take over and said they would need to make it legal. Unknowing about the daughter's intentions, Mary agreed. At the attorney's office, she was asked a few innocent questions as who the president is, what day is this, etc. The attorney then suggested Mary sign the papers, giving Jane legal guardianship over her mother's financial affairs. Mary had not been advised of the implications of guardianship, did not realize she was surrendering control of her monies, savings, retirement funds to her daughter. This dismayed and angered Mary for she had promised that none of her children would ever be in need. Mary knew that one daughter needed financial help.

Then, dissension arose among the daughters, each accusing the other of wanting more of the mother's estate both now and after Mary's death. A painful discussion among the girls resulted in Mary, in essence, writing a will that shared the estate equally among the daughters, but also limiting the monies that Mary could use for herself from her own resources. Of course, Mary had arranged her will so that any inheritance was equally distributed for her daughters. But Mary could no longer enjoy her monies, thwarted by the daughters who wanted to assure themselves of the most possible inheritance. The once peaceful and amicable daughters ended with jealousy and greediness for monies, with communications only by email, and with loss of sisterly relationships. In the months that followed, Mary became increasingly depressed – over the financial strictions and the loss of pleasant relationships among the three daughters.

In these days, almost any clever internet thief may attempt to gain control using the internet, telephone, or email.

1. I, personally, experienced this upon receiving an email stating that my bank account had been closed by my bank, for security reasons. Then, I was asked to reveal my name, address, personal information, kind of bank accounts, etc. The first time this happened I had almost completed the information, then erased it and called my bank. My account was not closed – it was an attempt by a "thief" to take control of my account; I received this request several times, with different urgent messages, trying to delve into my rather small checking account. Never open those warnings. Present them to the bank and block that sender.

PSYCHOLOGICAL AND EMOTIONAL ABUSE

Psychological abuse is the most common abuse suffered by the elderly. It is both verbal and emotional aggression. Verbal abuse includes such attacks as yelling, mocking, cursing, belittling, treating the person like a child or as incompetent, threatening, minimizing concerns, or making derogatory comments toward them. Emotional abuse is more subtle. It includes attitudes and feelings expressed toward the elderly spoken aloud or not, as ignoring them or their wishes, not liking to touch them, keeping the person isolated from family and friends, and making threatening gestures. Emotional abuse is in the feelings, attitudes, actions. Emotional abuse includes keeping the elderly in a room isolated from the rest of the home, of having visitors not shared with the elderly; in general, ignoring the presence of the elderly as if he/she were insignificant, or did not exist.

REACTIONS TO AND EFFECTS OF MALTREATMENT ON ELDERLY PERSONS

Many articles describe the presence of physical neglect and abuse that elderly persons endure and suffer. Many articles describe the emotional difficulties and physical demands of caring for the elder. The physical and emotional effects on caretakers of elderly is considered, and help is suggested for the caretaker. It is well accepted that the care for disabled elderly is often an overwhelming burden for a caretaker. Yet not much research addresses the effect of physical, and emotional abuse on elderly persons. There are only a few research studies that measure the effects of abuse on their lives, how it affects their disabilities, illnesses, sensory abilities, and emotional state.

There are, however, serious effects and consequences for the elderly – both for their physical health and psychological health. These effects are relative to and specific to the person, to the degree of health and disability and to their character, it is accepted that their length of life is shortened by abuse.

In a study (2008) that interviewed 5,777 adults aged sixty or older, researchers compared abused with non-abused elders. Eight years later, elders who reported being victims of psychological, physical, or sexual abuse were almost five times more likely than non-victimized to have been repeatedly abused during that time. The elder abuse victims reported higher rates of depression, general anxiety disorder and poorer health.[6] Also, post-traumatic disorder (PTSD) was correlated with elder mistreatment, lower income, poorer health, previous trauma, and requiring assistance with daily living tasks as dressing themselves. Moreover, there were significantly more deaths among the abused persons.

There are serious and lasting, even fatal, effects on the abused person. The immediate effects of physical or psychological effects are like post-traumatic disorder - difficulties eating, sleeplessness, impulse control, high blood pressure and the exacerbation of previous illnesses and weaknesses.[7]

In the case of Alice, who had fallen after surgery and

when no one was present to help her to the bathroom, she was left with a severe PTSD reaction. She suffered tremendous fear and anxiety, of ever again being placed in an assisted-living setting. She sobbed, preferring to die when once again she faced the possibility of a care institution as her illness progressed. She became more disabled, unable to get out of bed, and rather than enter assisted living, she employed caretakers for the help she needed.

Jane, who had generously given her home to her daughter, was shocked by the aggressive slap from her daughter. She cried from the sting and then was overwhelmed by her own anger and the angry slap of her daughter; Jane now refused to talk with her daughter. She would not eat or speak for several days.

Gradually becoming responsive to others – mostly because of the social and emotional support offered by other family members. Eventually, her daughter genuinely regretted the burst of anger and was overwhelmed by her own action toward her mother. An aside here, it would be important to protect Jane from another outburst of anger from her anxiety-ridden daughter by providing the daughter some help in caring for her mother, counseling if possible, and some free time for herself.

John, who was locked in his bedroom to keep him from wandering, was a seriously ill and cognitively impaired elder. He suffered a common reaction to medical neglect. He developed bedsores that became infected. At first, his reaction to the lack of care was to complain bitterly and angrily that he "hurt." And probably because of his level of dementia, the staff did not respond quickly to his pleas that he was suffering. His anger gradually turned into moaning; then he became depressed and non-responsive to the staff. Eating and sleeping were disturbed; he refused to talk or participating in receiving care. Then, given antidepressant medication, anger again erupted against the staff.

These are only a few of the types of reactions to abuse suffered by the elderly. Some other common reactions include unreasonable fears or suspiciousness of others and the events, uncommunicativeness, or unresponsiveness to others, lack of eye contact with others, helplessness, lack of interest in social contact, isolated, changes in behavior, and suicide.[8] Both physical and emotional abuse, once noted, are often repeated. The most troubling effect is the increased risk for premature death.

SUMMARY COMMENTS

This chapter has described the effects of the jolt to life that despoils the mood, damages the life, increases illnesses, and elicits suffering. The research has substantiated that as the elder becomes even older, he/she may anticipate an increasing possibility of abuse, neglect, or harm from another. We have seen that rape of an elder is considered less destructive to life, even though it is a criminal offense. Especially after the age of eighty, abuse increases when the elder is physically weaker, more ill, more disabled than earlier – more likely to need help or care, and much less able to protect the self. This chills the spirit.

It is the heartier and healthier that live longer. Yet they, too, become disabled and diseased. Stories that emerge from care institutions that "care for elders have been sobering. Illnesses of aging become a source and instigation for neglect and abuse. Some of the care-not-given borders on criminal neglect. Even sexual abuse of a patient is considered "a low-level problem that did not constitute actual harm or put residents in "immediate jeopardy." There are no real evaluations of elders living at home unless reported to doctors or police. Yet the statistics suggest that many elders suffer even more often and more serious than those ten-to-fifteen per cent abused in care institutions. Caretakers at home find little respite from the unusual difficult demands of an elder.

A smile from a passing stranger elicits a warm after-glow enriching our mood and coloring the air about us. As such, many interactions with others lighten the spirit with a sense of pleasure, adding to experiences that enrich our self and nurture life within us. Death is hastened by abuse; illness is accelerated and compounded; fears and anxiety are ever present; hope exists no more, a shattered memory. For the aged, it can be a world without compassion...or tender-heartedness...or empathy...

In our culture an idealization of youth, of individualism, of strength and intellectual acumen prevails. Medical advancements have prolonged heartiness and health. The aging process seems to extend youth and "middle-aged-ness have been extended for the elderly population.

These words are difficult to write. To face a future in which rejection of personhood for the elderly seems a high possibility, brings personal memories of lives and deaths of those I have known and loved. And of myself.

REFERENCES

1. Reuben Ng, Heather G. Allore, Trentalange, M, Monin JK, Levy BR (2015) Increasing negativity of Age Stereotype across 200 Years. Evidence from a Database of 400 Million Words. PLoS ONE 10(2): e0117086.) https.///doi.otg/10.1371/journal, pone,0117086 from 1810 too 2009.)

2. See the Sage Minder. https://sageminder.com/SeniorHealth/Issues/AgeDiscrimination.aspx

3. Please refer to the article by Acierno, R., Hernandez, M.S., Amstadter, A.B., Resnick, H.S. Steve, K., Muzzy, W. a & Kilpatrick, D.G. (2010) Prevalence and correlates of emotional physical, sexual and financial abuse and potential neglect in the United States: The National Elder Mistreatment Study. American journal of Public Health, 1002). 292-297.

4. The New York Times, Sunday, March 14, 2021. "To lift ratings, Nursing Homes Shroud Neglect" by Jessica Siler-Greenberg and Robert Gebeloff. Vol CLXX. No 58,997.

5. Cooper, C., Selwood, A., Blanchard, M., Walker, Z., Blizzard, R., * Livingston, G. (2009) "Abuse of people with dementia by family carers: representative cross-sectional survey. British Medical Journal 336, B155.

6. National Institute of Justice, "Insights on Adverse Effects of Elder Abuse," July 13, 2020, nij.ojp.ov: https://nij.ojp.gov/topis/artiles/insights-adverse-effects-elder-abuse

7. National Institute on Aging. Heeps://www.nia.nih.gov/health/elder-abuse

8. "Elder Abuse and Neglect" American Psychological Association. Please see www.apa.org/pi/aging.

CHAPTER SEVEN

The Loss Of Independence - Walking

The waters flow down the river, starting slowly from its source. Sometimes the river runs softly, calmly, flowing through a level spot of earth. Other times there are small and large rocks the water tumbles over, making the stream rough, irregular, and unpredictable; a sudden drop comes, creating an unexpected waterfall. At the end, the river joins the waters of the ocean, finding its natural end.

The flow of life is thus. Sometimes calm and easy, rough and tumble like the river, or traumata may strike, to affect the path of life. Then quiet.

WALKING AT 87

Walking around the campus those first days, I enjoyed the pleasant, almost forest-like environment. It seemed a quiet, inviting place to live. I gradually became more aware of people as they walked to and from various buildings.

The picture seemed different, somehow. And then it struck me – many, many of the people need help to move about. There were canes, walking sticks, walkers, wheelchairs, even motorized chairs. Walking was not easy for many, or most. Rarely did anyone walk without aid.

Was the joy of a walk – to be lost?

I find the day when I walk. Walking sets the mood for the day- breathing fresh air, listening to the whispers of the trees, watching the squirrels scamper in the quietness of the morning. All prepare my spirit for the oncoming day.

I walk before breakfast knowing that if I eat first, the walk is lost. I become busy with simple chores of the day – cleaning the kitchen, checking email, finishing undone tasks, whatever. Walking before breakfast graces the mood for the day.

Walking has changed for me, though. No longer do I fully enjoy the nature about me, the twittering of birds, clouds in the sky, or dew on the grass. Nor do I find myself turning inward, meditating on an unfinished thought, clarifying an event from the past day, thinking about tomorrow, or enjoying a spiritual "high" that walking sometimes blessed.

What has happened to the joy of walking? Gone is the spring in the step. Every step now demands awareness – not of the world about me, but of the next step to be taken. Caution! The concrete is uneven. Beware – a branch lays over the sidewalk, step carefully. Do not kick at that fallen acorn, you may surely fall. (I did). Every step now demands a correction of balance – walk straight ahead, not wavering like a drunken sailor. Watch your posture straighten the back, shoulders back, lift my knees, do not shuffle, listen for people coming from behind, walk straight so the oncoming person has room on the sidewalk...

I miss an ease of walking. The intense sense of being in touch with nature and the joy of that feeling – swinging my arms with each step, smiling at the playful squirrels, or musing on a new thought. The loss of elan spoiled by each measured step.

Yet, I walk. I want to walk. I love the walk. I like the sense of movement, marred though it is. I like the freshness of the air, the changing weather. I love being outside – away from the walls that enfold and enclose in the house. Keeping nature with me, my feelings are lifted, my spirit refreshed.

This is the story of many who have watched themselves grow older. Slowing down often begins earlier than expected, usually in the fifties. I wanted to understand the change in life that beset aging persons.

WALKING

One obvious characteristic of humans is the ability to walk on two feet. The infant may first crawl on all fours but watch the year old take its first step alone. She/he throws its arms into the air, jubilant, laughing in sheer exuberance with its success. Joy floods its face, even as it plumps onto the floor. This is independence!

The three-year-old toddler joyfully challenges a parent to catch him/her as it runs from mother in play – "catch me if you can!" Walking, running is fun. Independence grows with ability to walk. The freedom given through walking increases the child's growing sense of "I" – "I can move toward" or "I can move away."

Throughout childhood, games bring increasing strategies and complexities of movement – walking, running, hopping, skipping are practiced in many games. Ride develops with agility and speed. And contrariwise, feelings of shame and frustration accompany a child who cannot run as fast as others. In adolescence the grace of walking, of moving, becomes apparent in dance movements, in the complexity of motion required in sports as tennis, baseball, soccer, etc.

By adulthood, we have acquired a characteristic gait and speed of walking, moving quickly or slowly, stomping heavily or treading lightly, striding clumsily or gliding gracefully. We know and recognize each other partially by our style of movement. To walk, to be erect, is the pride of being human.

ONSET OF A SLOWER WALK

As we age, something happens. Walking becomes different. It may be an accident, a stroke, an illness or just aging. Posture, balance, and gait change. Some few retain a normal walk pattern throughout life – about ten percent by age eighty-five. Often just aging slows our walk, changes the pattern. In my instance, my balance was lost as an after-effect of antibiotic medication for an infection. The medicine damaged the nerves of the middle ear that help the sense of balance.

Physical changes begin in middle age and may be as

traumatic as changes of adolescence. Here is the beginning of aging, with gradual loss of muscle tone, changes in the nervous system - reflexes become slower, coordination suffers, misperceptions of near and far distances occur, etc. The pace of walking gradually slows, often overlooked until it becomes unavoidable. That day comes too soon.

In one study of walking of older persons, walking problems were detected in about 25 percent of persons at age sixty, and nearly 60 percent of those aged 80-84.[1] While yet in my fifties, I remember walking around campus, trying to match the pace of the college students. I could not keep up with them, not easily anyhow. Now I do not try. Movement difficulties come gradually and are often overlooked until unavoidable. Walking gait slows, oh so gradually, the day comes too soon when it is recognized as a problem.

Loss of mobility is common for older adults. About thirty percent of persons 65 years and older report difficulty walking three city blocks or climbing one flight of stars without becoming breathless. Approximately twenty percent require the use of a mobility aid to walk.

BALANCE

Balance is the harmony of the body. Balance, often taken for granted, may become a problem for the elderly. Balance, equilibrium, help us remain upright when standing and let us know where we are in relation to others and things in the environment. It helps us walk, run, and move without falling. Balance is controlled through signals to the brain from our eyes, the inner ear, and the sensory systems of the body (as skin muscle and joints). A sense of balance is required for walking.

A balance disorder is a condition that makes one feel unsteady and/or dizzy. One may stagger when walking or teeter or fall when trying to stand up. Other symptoms include dizziness or vertigo, falling, lightheadedness, faintness, or a floating sensation. Blurred vision or disorientation along with accompanying symptoms as nausea, diarrhea, changes in heart rate and blood pressure with fear, anxiety or panic may occur. Symptoms may come and go over short periods of time or last a long time. Loss of balance is not only a problem for the oldest old. Instead, like strength, agility and muscle mass, balance tends to start declining in midlife.[2]

Some individuals experiencing balance problems have an obvious medical diagnosis such as diabetes, Parkinson's disease or even a stroke that may be primary sources of the problem. However, diseases are not the only reason our sense and movements may be compromised. A history of injuries, such as concussions, ear infections or serious sprains and fractures, may contribute to the loss of balance control.

Want to check your balance? See if you can stand on one foot for a full minute. Thirty- to forty-year-old persons almost reach the minute mark; in the fifties, they may stand about 45 seconds; people in their sixties, forty seconds; in their seventies, 27 seconds, for folks over eighty, it was 12 seconds.

Even some medications may contribute to a loss of balance. I, personally, had this experience after given two antibiotic medications known to harm the nerves controlling balance. From that point on, my ability to maintain balance was permanently affected.

It is undeniable that balance is of prime importance for walking.

WALKING-BALANCE PROBLEMS

The style of walking reflects an habitual gait and posture that has developed during lifetime. Watch the five-year-old boy copy the walk of his father – bringing a smile to pleased parents. Many changes in walking style that occur in older adults are related to habitual stances that develop because of daily activities, and in turn, affect how they walk. For instance, I spent many year carrying heavy books and notebooks tucked under my left arm. Now, without noticing it all these years, my left shoulder is slightly lower, and I have less freedom of movement in that arm.

In a sample of noninstitutionalized older adults, thirty-five per cent had an abnormal gait. Walking problems were detected in about twenty-five percent of persons 70 to 74 four years of age and nearly six per cent of those 80-84 years old.

WALKING DIFFICULTIES

Walking problems are not an inevitable consequence of aging or illness. About 25 percent of elderly persons maintain good balance, posture, and walking ability throughout life. Many underlying medical conditions affect balance, posture, and walking. With appropriate medical intervention and physical therapy, many walking problems can be alleviated. With early identification of balance and walking problems, intervention may prevent dysfunction and loss of independence.[3]

One rather independent professional lady, aged 64, suffered a stroke that left her with weakness in the left arm and leg. Trying recommendations for physical therapy, she soon tired of the monotony of exercising. Thinking she could exercise without help, she asserted she had never been interested in athletics or exercise. So, she soon stopped therapy and exercising. Later, at the age of 85, she could hardly use her left leg at all, walked with a walker, or used a wheelchair. Now, trying to exercise more conscientiously, the possibility that she could regain use of her leg is guarded, affected by her increased age and physical weakness. Lost opportunities.

Balance and walking are multi-faceted. Illness, accidents, disabilities, even work habits may induce some walking disorders. Recovery may require several modes of treatment to restore, maintain, or improve the functional quality of walking. Generally, the earlier recovery efforts are undertaken, the better the possibility of effective rehabilitation. It is easy to postpone attending to walking problems for they may be considered temporary, seem unimportant, or just bothersome.

The following are some approaches to improvement of balance and walking style.

Medical evaluation: First and necessary in the order of treatment is a thorough medical evaluation of the possible causes affecting the balance and walking. The medical doctor should guide the person to effective adjunctive treatment.

Physical therapy: Physical therapy is designed to improve everyday functioning, provide a sense of confidence in walking, and increase the pleasure of movement itself. The foci of physical therapy are increases in the range of movement, strengthening muscles, and improving coordination and balance. Often this involves teaching the muscles new movements and increasing muscle strength.

Tai Chi: *Tai* Chi is called "Meditation in Motion." It consists of mind-body exercises rooted in traditional Chinese medicine and philosophy. Coordinated sequences of exercises are performed with concentration and inner calmness that affect both balance and walking movements. This inner calm with movement improves energy and sustains and improves health.[4]

Since 1996, there have been investigations concerning the effectiveness of Tai Chi on the health and wellbeing of older adults. The exercises are not strenuous. The aim is to strengthen, to relax, and to integrate the physical body and mind, and to improve health. Research has shown that Tai Chi exercises may lead to improved balance, reduced fear of falling, increased strength, better functional mobility, greater flexibility and increased psychological well-being.

LOSS OF INDEPENDENCE: The loss of walking brings the loss of physical independence. As jubilant as the youngster finding that it can move alone, can walk by itself, delighted in the sense of independence, so demeaning is the oldster discovering he or she can no longer walk alone. The sense of independence is shattered. The person may feel demeaned, of lesser ability now. Sadness comes. Anger at oneself or others may rise. Help is needed; and help is often right there.

I recall Murray, a gentleman who had a stroke that left him needing a wheelchair. To facilitate getting around the environment, he chose a motorized chair. A well-liked eighty-five-year-old gentleman, Murray wheeled into the dining room, pulled up to the table, and then with some effort, he stood and announced, "I am ashamed. I am ashamed to have to use a wheelchair." Others in the dining room, clapped for him. They appreciated and empathized with his statement for they, too, had faced times when their lack of independence affected them. He was ashamed, no longer the whole man he once thought he was. Shame makes us want to hide, embarrassed by our disabilities.

Losing mobility has profound social, psychological, and physical repercussions. Meeting with friends becomes difficult, almost impossible, without help. Ordinary tasks, as shopping or preparing food become problems. The sense of self is changed, pride is injured. And then anger may come – anger at the disabled status, anger that others want to help. A sensitivity that other recognize the impairment of "not being able" to manage everyday actions stings one's pride.

ACCEPTANCE AND ADJUSTMENT

Foremost in managing the compelling difficulties of the loss of mobility is acceptance of the loss. To be able to say, "I cannot walk. Now what can I do?" is the beginning of recovery. Easy as the words are to write, the time for acceptance may take longer. It is a gradual emotional acceptance to acknowledge, "I cannot walk" or "I cannot walk as well as I did." Relevant to the severity of the physical change, a mourning for lost abilities may take time to accept the reality. Mourning brings a sense of sadness, grief for the lost ability, unhappiness or even anger. Depression may linger heavily, until the person becomes determined to encounter the disability, to keep a spirit of life, to maintain a sense of self and identity. Mobility was an important ability; mobility does not define the person.

Susan, age eight-six, had suffered a stroke, leaving one side of her body stiff and mostly unusable; then discovering that Parkinson's Disease had set in, she was sad, downhearted. Plucky as she normally was, she set about to do as much as she could for herself. Not only did she become an avid listener to books on tape, but she also began to practice the piano again, a talent that had been unused for some years. No, she did not recover all her movement or skill, but a zest for life was recovered.

Adaptation means making changes to facilitate movement in the home or hospital. More significantly, alterations in expectations of oneself comes gradually as actions are tried, perhaps discarded, as new actions are found. As experience of the limits of capabilities comes, the person says to him or herself, "This is me. I cannot do this; I can do this." It is important to challenge the difficulties of lost movement, to test the limit of impairment, to counter the disability with the courage and effort that can be mustered.

Even more challenging are alterations in daily habits and life patterns. Daily habits may change. It may be more difficult to pour a cup of coffee, get to the bathroom, get dressed or undressed. Each daily habit may have to be adjusted to account for the physical that has occurred. In other words, old behaviors are dropped, and with practice, new behaviors are found to manage wants, needs, or desires. With success in learning new behaviors, a sense of competence returns. Well-being, even happiness, again finds its place in life.

With the adjustment to the changed life circumstances, comes the recognition that others - family and friends - must also change their attitude, expectation, and behavior toward us. Patience and making allowance for other's difficulties in adjusting to changes in abilities, interactions and relationships are necessary. It may take time for the emotional closeness to return as new and different behaviors are acknowledged by others. It will be necessary to say, "I can do this myself." Or "Could you please help me with this?" Patience, and calm observations will help as family, friends or caretakers adjust to the changes.

Others may overlook, or deny, the changes compelled by the disability. In one instance, a patient, Emma, reported that her friend had completely denied her disabilities. Emma had lived alone in the independent living community for a couple years. She had hearing problems, was almost blinded by visual difficulties and her physical abilities were diminished because of a stroke that left her unable to walk without a walker. Her neighbor of two years angrily confronted Emma's caretaker with an accusation, saying, "there is really nothing wrong with Emma. Is there?" The neighbor claimed that Emma was faking her illnesses. Such attitudes complicate social interactions and relationships even more.

In such instances, the disabled person is compelled to provide *allowances* for those who do not comprehend effects of disabilities, who mistakenly are unthoughtful in expectations of others. Importantly an admirable approach for those with whom the person interacts is a resurgence of politeness in interactions with the ailing person and with others. "Yes, please, thank you, could you, etc." Politeness, at least, is an acknowledge of the person's capability and integrity.

SUMMARY COMMENT

Of all the difficulties encountered facing the aging person, the loss of freedom of mobility ranks among the most severe. The loss of walking complicates the sense of "I" first learned by the two-year-old toddler. The person can no longer deny some dependence on others. There are many causes for walking and balance difficulties which almost seem inescapable in age. Seventy-five percent of individuals over seventy-five years of age have walking problems. Acceptance, adaptation, and adjustment to the difficulties need be met with an actively accepting and challenging attitude. The elan of life can be maintained.

ADDENDUM

HELPFUL DEVICES FOR WALKING

There are many devices that provide stability and support for those who have difficulty in walking. These vary from the simple cane to motorized scooters which enable a person to ride easily in the environment – both indoors and outside. Some device to aid walking is reportedly used by over fifty per cent of adults over seventy-five years.

Walking Canes: An assistive cane approximately waist high and with a handle or formed hand grip on the upper end. It is used as a mobility aid. It helps redistribute weight from a leg that is weak or painful, improve stability by increasing the base of support and provides tactile information about the ground to improve balance. Some lesson in its use is advisable for it is easy to trip over the cane itself.

Walking Sticks: This is a rod or stick, usually chin high, used to aid walking and/or hiking. Usually there are two walking sticks, one for each hand that permits some rhythm in the walk. I favor walking sticks for posture is not bent forward, as it is with a cane or walker.

Crutch: A staff or support stick designed to fit under the arm. These are often used in pairs by a physically injured or disabled person to aid walking. The support comes from the shoulders.

Walker: This a frame of wood or metal, usually with small wheels, or rubber tipped feet, used for support in walking. There are many varieties of walkers, which often including a seat for resting.

Motorized chair: this is a power operated vehicle with an electric motor designed to aid elderly or disabled individuals with some movement, confidence and independence in and outside the home.

REFERENCES

1. Pirker, Walter and Katschenlager Regina. 2016. "Gait disorders in Adults and the elderly: A Clinical Guide" https://pubmed.ncbi.nih.gov;27770207/

2. NIH National Institute on Dearness and other Communication Disorders (NIDCD) https:/www/mode/mo/gpvea;tijba;ace-disorders.

3. Salzman, Booke, MD 2010. "Gait and Balance Disorder in Older Adults" Ann Fam Physician 2010 July 1 812(1) 61-68.

4. Kuramoto, Alice M., PhD, RN, BC, FAAN. "Therapeutic benefits of Tai Chi Exercise: Research Review" 2006. Wisconsin Medical Journal, 2006. Vol. 105, No. 7, pp. 42-46.

CHAPTER EIGHT

Falling What Makes Falling Happen So Often?

*The water rushes on, full of energy...without warning
it rushes down a cliff...splashes and whirls around...
gradually slows and resumes its journey...*

INITIAL CONSIDERATIONS

As we also do. Balance is the harmony of the body.
Losing balance feels awkward. Stumbling, dragging one's
feet, grabbing onto a chair or wall gives support. Harmony
is lost. It is an important factor in falls. Balance requires the
coordination of muscles, bones, eyes, hearing, heart, and
blood vessels – all must work normally to sustain upright
posture - good balance. Harmony may at times be affected
by the environment, as provoked by unexpected noises,
stones in the pathway, but mostly arises from feelings or
thoughts, that evoke a loss of bodily synchrony. Impaired

balance may result from illnesses, physical disabilities, or often psychological factors as with interrupted attention, emotional intrusions, or depression.

The process of aging flowing through our physical self is often, at first, unnoticed. Little actions gradually come to attention when an habitual movement fails. For instance, in reaching for a glass of wine, the person touches the glass – almost reaches it -misses - and the wine flows across the white tablecloth. Or trying to place a cup on the table, the older person mistakenly judges the distance, places the cup on the edge of the table, and it spills. What an embarrassment! The self-observation is, "Oh, I have to be careful."

These examples demonstrate the effect of changing perceptions, of spatial misjudgments. Our arms do not have the same reach, our vision misjudges distance, or we fumble in our intent. Another illustration – buttons become difficult to fit into the buttonhole; it seems our fingers are not as dexterous as once. To button the shirt takes more precise attention. With effort, we gradually adjust to our changed capabilities. We learn to be a little more attentive.

EFFECTS ON WALKING - FALLING

Perceptual changes and these unnoticed slowing of motor movements affect our walking, making balance and physical grace difficult. We walk more slowly; the width of step becomes smaller. We scrutinize the unevenness of the sidewalk, walk around corners more slowly, all to avoid a misstep. And falls are dangerous for our body is more fragile, even skin seems thinner. Falling is hurtful and can cause serious injury. It seems the older we are, the more damage a fall brings.

Walking down steps may become fear-provoking. Imagine a two-year-old child enjoying the thrill of walking up the stairway. Now recall the difficulty he/she has in coming down. At first, the child sits down on the step, and then gingerly scoots down one step at a time, carefully sitting on each step. For the aged person, walking down often seems unsafe, there is only empty space ahead unless there is a banister to grasp. Walking downwards provokes anxiousness even when stepping off a curb with no support available.

The report of the National Councill on Aging states that falls are the leading cause of fatal and non-fatal injuries for older citizens.[1] One in every three Americans over 65 fall each year; twenty-seven thousand adults die each year from a fall; 2.8 million injuries are treated in emergency departments annually, over 800,000 are hospitalized. In 2017 falls were the leading cause of accidental death for Floridians age 55 and older. Half of these deaths occurred to those over the age of 85 years.[2] The anxieties and fears of falling that perfuses the older person is easily understood. It is a healthy fear that alerts the person to danger.

CAUSES OF FALLING

The causes of falling are many.[3] First is a general decline in physical fitness that makes walking slower, less sure. The walk becomes slower, the steps shorter, and the gait smaller. A misstep, losing balance, and falling becomes easier.

Loss of balance is the important factor in falls. Balance requires the coordination of muscles, bones, eyes, the balance nerve in the middle ear, heart, and blood vessels – all must work normally to sustain good balance. The harmony may be affected by the environment but mostly from feelings, thoughts, or bodily loss of synchrony. Impaired balance may result from illnesses, physical disabilities, or psychological factors as attentional factors or depression – all contributing to the possibility of a fall.

Many older persons who fall cannot get up. Sometimes this inability surprises the older person who had not realized the loss of strength that had occurred over time. One gentleman (age 82) who was active in driving and managing his life, fell while tripping on a rug in his apartment. He could not raise himself from the floor. To his amazement, he had to call the caretaker who lifted him to is feet in one easy motion.

It is estimated that almost 47% of non-injured fallers are unable to get off the floor without help. For those who lie on the floor for more than an hour, half will be dead within six months. The "long lie" is a result of physical weakness, illness, or social isolation.[4]

The place of falls varies with the situation. Falls on the stairs or in the bathroom are relatively rare. Men tend to fall outside, perhaps in the garden, women, in the house. In care residences, many falls occur on the way to the bathroom. Often enough, falls are the result of a miscalculation of the elders as in doing something "in a hurry," testing abilities, or overextending their present capabilities.

Some medications have side effects that contribute to falling are those that effect the person with drowsiness, dizziness, or low blood pressure. Cognitive impairment, as in Alzheimer's disease, is a major risk factor for falls; actually, the risk of falls is doubled with dementia.[5] Even a momentary loss of attention can be disastrous. Environmental factors as loose carpets or slippery surfaces, poor lighting, clutter, or stairways are but a few of the unanticipated factors that evoke falling.

A friend once asked to join me on my usual morning walk. As politely as possible, I refused her request, telling her that "I cannot walk and talk at the same time." My balance is unstable and walking itself, demands concentration. Frustrated, I had to admit that I could not do two things at once.

There are interesting research studies showing how divided attention may provide some indication of susceptibility to falling. Research aimed at evaluating the predictability of falls in older persons have investigated the gait of elderly persons when walking is complicated by an additional task. The task involved "walking while talking" for it had been observed that elderly persons would slow down or stop walking while talking.[6] Elderly persons were asked to walk 40 meters and to carry out a simple cognitive problem as reciting the letters of the alphabet or a more complex task, recite alternate letters of the alphabet. The time to complete the walk was recorded. In a twelve-month follow-up period, the time taken for the walk and halting the walk while talking, were found to be a significant predictor of falls.

While the reader may smile at this example, there is much research that dual task requirements are predictive of falls. The common jest of not being able to "do two things at once" is finding support.

The elder person now walks slower, with a learned carefulness and cautiousness for each step. This cautiousness often is termed "fear of falling" in the elderly. However, the fear of falling is an innate reaction to danger; it becomes problematic only when undue anxiety and preoccupation interfere with desired activity.

REFERENCES

1. These statistics are gleaned from the National Council of Aging, Sept. 27, 2020. "Falls Prevention Facts." https:/// www.ncoalorg/news/resources-for0reporterls/ge-the=facts,/ falls-prevention-facts/

2. Nikki Ross, May 29, 2019. "Falling is the leading cause of death for Florida's elderly. Medical Press htts://medicalpress.co/ news/2019-050falling-death-florida-elderly-html

3. Marie Solitto, "Things that Cause the Elderly to Fall: I June 9, 2020. Mobility (https://www.agingcaree.com/topics/128/ mobility

4. Stephen Lord, Catherine Sherrington, and Hylton B. Menz. 2000. Falls in Older People: Risk Factors and Strategies for Prevention. Cambridge: Cambridge University Press. (ISBN 0-521-58964-9 (p/b).

5. G. Mulley. 2001. "Falls in older people." Journal of the Royal Society of Medicine. Apr. 94(4) 202.

6. J. Verghese, H. Buschke, L. Viola, et al. "Validity of divided attention tasks in predicting falls nn older individuals: aa preliminary study. 2002. Journal of the American Geriatrics Society, 50 (2002) 1572-6.

CHAPTER NINE

Independence Lost The Question Of Automobile Driving

What is pushing the river...is it the slope of the land?
Too many rocks? Too many curves?? making the water
crash...has the river changed...it seems to be entering
into a larger splash of water...the river is changing?

THE AUTOMOBILE

Freedom is sitting in a car and driving off – to the grocery store or the mall – or to a restaurant for a tasty meal, or even better for a weekend in the mountains with your partner. Leaving responsibilities behind, for a short ride or even better for a weekend far from the telephone, the bills awaiting payment, the uninvited visitor, brings deep relaxation to the mood. Packing suitcases, placing children in the back seats, driving off for the week is exhilarating. How vividly I remember my first experience driving an automobile from Ohio to Colorado. My first teaching job, and alone. After bidding farewell to many family members, I drove off. Alone. Excited. Free. Now, I wonder how far I could or would drive alone?

The automobile has brought increased familiarity with the immediate environment, knowing one's way around the city to find the doctor, the dentist, the best shopping areas, and the home of your friend. Time saving, energy saving, life invigorating. It is the preferred travel for vacations - to national parks, to visiting relatives and friends, to acquaintance with the country.

The loss of license to drive an automobile seems a final insult to the person who cherishes the freedom of movement. Many folk remain physically capable to drive a car, even though walking has become difficult - cherishing driving as a sign of autonomy, of independence. Although the older driver has safer driving behavior than younger persons, there are more automobile accidents among older drivers due to the physical problems brought by aging.

In 2019 there were more than 44 million drivers aged sixty-five and older. This year, almost 6,907 older adults were killed in motor vehicle accidents; and more than 257,000 were treated in emergency hospitals for automobile accidents.[1] Those over 75 years of age have higher death rates from accidents than middle-aged drivers. Male drivers have substantial higher death rates than females.

Do the elderly decide for themselves?

It is not unusual that the older-old person makes the choice not-to-drive. Often it may be due to visual or hearing losses, or to other illnesses or disabilities that make driving difficult. Other times, a capable person simply experiences that driving has become difficult.

Driving gradually demands more attention. The older driver finds it more difficult to get in the car, to reach the pedals, or the correct button. More caution is needed in traffic, travelling slower, watching the flow of traffic. For the older-old person, a caution about driving slowly comes. Many choose not to drive. I happened to be watching a friend park his automobile, walk quickly toward me, and state firmly, "That is the last time I drive the car anywhere!" He almost had an accident. That was proof to him he did not want fear of an accident ever again.

I recall my mother (age 85 years) being reluctant to have any passengers with her. She became cautious about a possible accident, about responsibility for any other person in the car when she was driving. This increasing reluctance to drive is the warning for themselves that many elderly accept. They choose not to drive, to use other resources.

A Boy Scout leader, Mike (age 68) was taking a carload of boys to a camp. Driving along, and coming to an irregular railroad track, he slowed while on the track, and as he did, the car stalled. On the track. A train was coming -unexpectedly? Or was he trying to "beat" the train? That answer was never to be known for the train hit the car, killing him and the boys, instantly.

The loss of license to drive an automobile seems a final insult to the person who cherishes the freedom of movement. It encaptures feelings of many folk who remain physically capable to drive a car, even though walking has become difficult - cherishing driving as a last sense of independence. Although, the older driver has safer driving behavior than younger persons, there are more automobile accidents among older drivers due to the physical problems brought by aging.

Somehow now, the car does not call me as strongly as it did...I do not go out as often. The last time I hit the curb when I turned. I no longer go for an afternoon drive in the countryside alone. Now I prefer to have someone with me. Freeways demand more attention. Even talking takes my attention from the road.

When adult children make the decision?

Often enough, it may be an adult child that decides a parent should not be driving. Fears for possible accidents, about driving skills, simply safety. Often, the adult child is correct, not always. The most important consideration for the driver-parent is not age alone, nor health factors that do not interfere with the manipulation of the automobile. It is related to the health, physical environment, frequency of driving, and ability to drive.

One family with an elderly mother had a family meeting to discuss mother's driving. The oldest child wanted to refuse Mother any driving possibilities. Mother lived alone in her home in a country town and used the automobile rarely – to go to church or the grocery store. A discussion among the seven children included questions as: "What does mother want?" "Who thinks she should not drive?" "Where, how far does she drive?" She wanted, felt she needed to be able to have her car. The children voted in her favor.

One day the mother telephoned a child. "Can I drive to the store to get an ice cream cone?" She had listened to her children, aware of their concerns for her safety, and submitted to their wishes for her – not only for her own safety, but also to remain in good relationship with her children.

One eighty-two-year-old lady had her license taken away by her children. This infuriated her. She had just completed a program ordered by the Court because she had been given a traffic ticket for weaving about on the road; she had been inebriated. The children, fearful of continued driving or accidents, had done the thoughtful and protective act for their mother. The mother sulked for a while, then decided to take the State's test for a new license to drive. She passed on the third try; purchased another car.

WHEN SHOULD THE DRIVER'S LICENSE BE RELINQUISHED?

First, good health is a prerequisite for driving. Any health condition that requires medications that could impair driving ability is the first sign to stop driving. For instance, antianxiety drugs, narcotics and sleeping pills affect the recognition of situations and impair the immediacy of reaction time. This suggests that your foot and leg may react too slowly to press on the brakes in a timely manner. A host of other health conditions also impair driving ability such as visual problems or hearing difficulties. Muscular stiffness or injury, as a stiff neck that makes it difficult to turn your head rapidly, impair driving. Physical conditions as spastic movements, muscle stiffness, involuntary contractions, uncontrollable jerking, twitching movements, or other muscular deficiency, may interfere with the control of movement, and accuracy or speed of reaction – as in the need to quickly engage the brakes of the automobile. All of these are signs to request your doctor's counsel about the decision to continue driving.[2]

There are other indications that it is time to stop driving an automobile. The National Institute on Aging suggests that an older person can decide when it is time to stop driving by answering the following questions:[3]

Do other drivers often honk at me?

Have I had some accidents – even if they were only "fender benders"?

Do I get lost or confused even on streets I know?

Do cars or people walking seem to appear out of nowhere?

Do I get distracted while driving?

Have family, friends or my doctor said they are worried about my driving?

Do I have trouble staying in my lane?

Do I have trouble moving my foot between the gas and the brake pedals or sometime confuse the two?

Have I been pulled over by a police officer about my driving?

Other warnings of unsafe driving include answers to these questions:

Do you tend to become lost or confused while driving in familiar areas?

Do you have difficulty in parking? Do you easily remember where you parked the car?

Do you have a history of negligent driving behavior?

Does talking take your attention away from driving?

These are signs of possible difficulties. To compel oneself to evaluate how difficult or arduous driving is becoming demands self-awareness and concern for others. Often enough, a family member will suggest that it is time for an aging person to stop driving – before the aging person had given thought to surrendering driving the automobile. An aging person may scare him/herself because of a close call while driving. And the difficulty of driving at nighttime gives one pause about driving. I recently moved to the city in which I now live. Driving at night is treacherous. I have difficulties finding my way home in daylight; in the dark it is almost impossible.

Life without freedom of an automobile

Adjusting to life without a car can be challenging. Losing a sense of freedom and independence that driving a car brings, elicits many feelings – some shame, some irritability, some worries, some anger, and often depression. One study followed 4,300 adults over age 65.[4] For those who could no longer drive, there was a drastic reduction in social participation. The author reports: "Older adults who remain engaged in social life report being in better health, experience lower mortality risk over time, and have lower rates of depression, dementia and other cognitive impairment." The loss of driving not only brought a depressive reaction to the loss of independence, but also the loss of friends and social contact. The results of sixteen published studies found that seniors tended to show poorer health after they stopped driving, particularly, depressive symptoms.[5] However, the studies could not distinguish among the many factors affecting the health of seniors. For instance, was there a decrease in health that inhibited driving or did increased health problems follow the loss of driving?

Transportation mobility is often crucial for self-esteem, social roles, and continued social participation, as church attendance. Consideration and planning that enable a continuation of social activities would ease some distress following the loss of driving and assure a continuation of social relationships.

REFERENCES

1. National Highway Traffic Safety Administration, 2020. "Motor Vehicle Safety" Center,

2. There are several resources for information about elderly person and automobile driving. For instance: Federal Highway administration Department of Transportation. Highway Statistics 2017. Washington, DC, FHWA. 2018. https:/www.fhwa.dot.gov/ppolicyinformation/statistics/2017/ Also at https://crashsstats.nhtsa.dotgov/Api/Public/ViewPublicatio/812691

3. National Institute on Aging. 2020. Older Drivers. https:///www.nia.nih.gov/health/older-drivers

4. The research by Teja Pristaec, as reported by Lisa Rapaport, 2016. "When seniors stop driving, social isolation looms," Health News.

5. Owsley C. Driver capabilities in transportation in an aging society: a decade of experience. Technical Papers and Reports from a Conference: Bethesda, MD. Nov 7-9, 1999. Washington, DC, Transportation Research Board, 2004.

Chapter Ten

Grandparents – Parents – Grandchildren And Their Importance

The waters once roiling, now quiet and serene. A single stream, a lonely stream. Clear, warm water flows, moving along to merge with the large, timeless water ahead; from shallow waters of old are collected and shed. Streams merge, sometimes wild rushes of water enter the passive stream. Not storms, not really. Just rough passage to the end...timelessness is visible ahead.

IMPORTANCE OF FAMILY

Family provides the primary bond throughout life. From childhood on, personal identity has been encompassed in family bonds – yes, even though at times untied, denied, or lost. Mother, father, sister, or brother are self-identifications developed within a family context. Later, life pathways provide other ways of thinking of one's self - as mother, father, typist, doctor, teacher, secretary, soldier, bricklayer, housewife, etc. These are roles, parts played in life and in the culture. Family is basic; its effects pop up, to direct the selection of choices, development of friendships, guidance of morality.

The final stages of the Summing Up and Encore Phases are here. Life has been reviewed, integrated into the pattern of life, bringing a deeper understanding of the years. A place of rest, of leisure resides within. The elderly watched their families grow from the early days of childhood to adulthood, parenthood, and retirement. Grandchildren and great-grandchildren bring strong awareness of the continuity of life recognized in the familiarity of appearance, of style of speech, in manner of walking, in random gestures. Continuity.

The *nuclear family,* including parents and children, constitutes the core of culture. First used as a term in sociological studies in 1941, the nuclear family has been the central unit of societies over many centuries. Mother, father, and child are icons of cultural continuity, represented in cultural lore for over four thousand years, grouped by nature itself.[1] The family unit, the primary focus of emotional life, has been, and is, considered the most important source of happiness and satisfaction. The idealized nuclear family develops a cohesive bond in which there is a sense of belonging, and an affection for each other. In this unit, members care for each other, are guided by values and standards, and support members suffering stress.

The *extended family* includes grandparents, aunts, uncles, cousins who may share the bonding, depending upon the quality of interaction and warmth of relationships among the members. The extended family can make significant contributions to the emotional and economic welfare of each generational unit. The present popular search for ancestral lineage represents the ongoing interest in the continuity of life and identity – and possible ancient contributions to the present quality of personhood.

The role of grandparents has changed over the centuries. In earlier centuries, the "extended family" was the norm, especially in agrarian cultures. Commonly an older child continued living in the family home and cared for the wellbeing of the elders and children. Shared homes were necessary to provide housing and nurturance for all. This is continuing now in economically deprived families. In the "good old days" washing clothes, transportation, even social life seemed simpler, more direct. Presently, the ideal family appears to be that each generation lives separately, thus avoiding the schism that provides for different views of life that arise between generations. The rapid changes brought over the last two hundred years by scientific advances, technology, automation, and communication have also separated the generations from each other. "And now, about twelve per cent of elderly are living longer, the spread of generations is not just three generations, but four, even five.[2]

Grandparents held a significant role in the family – in control of family activities until in older age, when responsibility was surrendered to the younger generation. Even so, the family focus was the wellbeing of the grandparents, granting them services and honoring their wishes. Within the nuclear family, grandparents are not part of the household. Grandparents have been marginalized, omitted from many nuclear family activities. One result of the emphasis on the nuclear family is that families became more "child-centered."

In the present, the role of grandparents within the family has not only shifted, but it has also become variable. Relationships are now defined by the needs and the wishes of the grandchild's home. Parental separations by divorce, LGBT parents, and economic needs, are but a few of conditions that contribute uncertainties and variations to traditional family roles.

In 2020 about seventy percent of Americans more than 65 years old had at least one grandchild, becoming endowed with the new status as grandparents at about forty-five years of age. Approximately twenty percent, or sixty-four million, of family households in the U.S. are now extended family households in which one or more grandparent lives within the nuclear family. About five million children under age 18 now reside in grandparent-headed households; about twenty percent of these children have neither parent present in the home. According to Pew research in 2014, only 46 per cent of children under the age of eighteen lived with two married heterosexual parents, as compared to 73% in 1970. These are drastic changes affecting family relationships, family identity, and family expectations.

We now look at some of the ongoing relationships between parents, children, and grandchildren. How do grandparents fit into the family? What part of family life do the elderly enjoy? What are the practical and psychological relationships that emerge in our "aging" culture? Grandchildren are soon followed by further generations as fourth and fifth generations are soon enough present as well.

PARENTS AND CHILDREN AND GRANDCHILDREN

The quality of the physical and psychological bond with children developed during childhood continues into adult years and, by extension, to grandchildren. As children themselves become parents, feelings toward their children reflect the quality of attachment and depth of bonding of the generations.

The cohesive bond of families is an ideal. Yes, individuals have deep, sometimes long-lasting jealousies, angers, envies that break the once cohesive bonds and last a lifetime. Others experience lifelong support and caring of family members. Those embedded feelings, molded by stress and trauma, often enough separate members from each other, destroying trust and confidence. Many are the families, the siblings, torn apart by jealousies over money or other signs of love given by the parents. In other family groups, the stress, anxieties and/or trauma may deepen the bond, the empathy, and care for each other.

We discuss a few specific patterns that arise between adult child and elderly parent,

GRANDPARENT MOVES INTO THE FAMILY

Dorothy and her husband, John, gladly accepted her mother, Annie, into their home when Annie (74 years old) developed hypertension and balance problems. It seemed an ideal situation for the mother was given a large room with an "ell" extension that provided for some kitchen appliances. Both seemed content and happy with the arrangement, mother was well taken care of, and Dotty and John maintained some privacy.

Yet, even so, situations often arise in which the parent and daughter become unhappy with each other. One day Dorothy came home to find her seventy-four-year-old mother scrubbing the kitchen floor on her knees, the old-fashioned way. distraught at the sight of her old mother doing such a difficult task, Dorothy cried out in dismay and anger. Annie was hurt, sad for trying to be helpful. This incident remained unresolved between them. Yes, even at times when the daughter and mother love each other dearly, situations of misunderstanding may arise.

Dorothy had good intentions. She wanted her mother with her. She wanted to help her mother, to take care of her, to protect her, and to provide comfort. Annie, in turn, living alone after her husband had died, was accustomed to household responsibilities, and in control over her own home and activities. Annie wanted to belong, and to help in her new home.

No matter how well mother and daughter loved each other, were familiar with each other's behavior and personality traits, moving together is a new, strange, situation for all – whether to the parent's home or to the daughter's home. If the adult child also has children present in the home, increased elements of unpredictability are present. For both family and "grandmother," daily schedules are altered, expectations are new, changes are necessitated. Adjustment often is more difficult than expected and will take more time than anticipated. The first days together are exploratory for family and grandmother as new habits are being patterned.

When grandmother moves into the home there are changes in the family's space. "Home" changes for all. Once private space now becomes shared space. The addition of grandmother may temporarily alter the sense of comfort and intimacy for the family, and grandmother may feel as intruding. When grandmother arrives, help her feel comfortable, show her the special places in the home – as her room in the home, Dad's office, his personal space, son's room, and his computer, etc.

There are changes in the family's times. Daily times as rising for the day, mealtimes, or bedtimes may be altered. Family schedules for the day may change. Alteration of the next day's events may be necessary. The family may be eager, reluctant, or anxious for the change; grandmother may be reluctant, fearful, insecure. Adaptations come with effort; it is well to discuss the possible changes prior to her arrival.

Grandmother's sense of security will be helped when she is aware of the family's schedule as well as any activity for herself for the next day.. It is also helpful to prepare grandmother for her own appointments with beauty salon or medical work for the week; then, in two days you have an appointment; then, tomorrow, then, gently, "Do you remember?" "Today is special.". Sharing the knowledge of special, oncoming family events for the next week is especially helpful, even if it must be repeated over and over

A reminder here: Obstinacy in the grandparent may arise from a sense of the daughter's fears, anxiety or reluctance, as the research suggests. Or it may come from a grandmother's fear, a need to be in charge to affirm herself as a real person with wishes and control of life. A calmer mood, a calm discussion may now prevail over the anxiety of the grandmother and may quiet the anxious expectations of the daughter.

THE ADULT CHILD AS PARENT; ROLE REVERSAL?

When aging sets upon the grandparents, adult child(ren) are often faced with caring for, and providing for, the physical and psychological care of the surviving parent – and it is usually the adult daughter and the elderly mother. Probably because the female is more prepared for caretaking responsibilities, and more in tune with the needs that arise, much more is written about Grandmother – Adult daughter interactions. Communication problems come that can create friction and stress between them.

The elderly parent (elderly mother or father) dealing with the loss of physical strength and ardor, with sensory-motor problems, with memory or cognitive lapses finds herself dependent, often needing basic help as dressing, bathing, etc. Letting another do those activities that once were so private is at first difficult, often resisted. The parent seeks to retain a sense of her/his personhood. Even while generally grateful for the love and care, a sese shame, self-anger and/or resistance driven by the helplessness, gives way to the need, then acceptance and gratefulness for the care given through the automatic response of "no" or apparent stubbornness.

Communication may become difficult when adult-child assumes the care of an adult parent and elderly parent. They are caught in a generational schism. The adult child, often with her own responsibilities for work, children, house and whatever else, assumes additional responsibilities and care for the elderly mother. And it usually is a daughter or daughter-in-law that carries most of the burden of care as the adage states, "A son is a son until he takes a wife. A daughter is a daughter the whole of her life."

In addition, there is a generational schism in talking, and in communication between mother and daughter. There is a fall back with the daughter when she reverts to talking to her mother as if she were a child under her responsibility. For instance, the mother often enough will speak in a tone of voice used when telling children what to do. "You have a doctor's appointment today." "I am not going," is the reply. Often enough, a suggestion by the adult child comes after consideration of the problem. To the parent, it comes as surprise and as a order. Permit me here to remind the reader that strong determination (stubbornness) and resilience are two characteristics of those persons in the Summing Up and Encore Phase.

In approaches to calm the mother's resistance, many suggestions are given for talking to the aged mother, as what to say, how to address difficult subjects, how to convince the elderly parent to submit or respond more positively to the daughter's perspective are suggested as. Not many considerations are given to the elderly parent's feelings or views.

The elderly parent (elderly mother or father) dealing with the loss of physical ardor, with sensory-motor problems, often with memory or cognitive lapses, seek to retain a sense of themselves through the automatic response of "no" or apparent stubbornness. Yet, if given the opportunity to make the choice suggested, would accept the choice offered.

Often enough, while a suggestion by the adult child may come after much sober consideration of the problem. To the parent, it comes as a surprise and as an order. Permit me to remind the reader that strong determination (stubbornness) and resilience are two characteristics found with those in the Summing Up and Encore Phase. These reflect a need to retain a sense of self on the elder parent, of control of one's life, of being a person.

An elder mother may recognize the tone of voice, an authoritative, tense attitude, she receives when her adult child speaks to her. It may well reflect her/his own manner of control and response to children when the children were young. The daughter may not be especially aware that she has adopted the elderly mother's authoritative voice when speaking. "Parenting the parents" has almost become an expectation of adult child-elderly parent interactions. As may have been true with the child, the reflection in tone of voice, expression of feelings, and anticipation of obedience, coming from the adult child now provokes resistance or anger in the parent.

The challenge is that the elder parent is now compelled to learn new and different ways of responding, to avoid the role of child, and to model alternate types of response for, and to, the adult daughter. The elderly mother must learn to ask questions as "what will happen?" "Is it necessary? "Do I have to?"

The authoritative statement of the daughter, although given with all good intention, is heard as an infringement upon the integrity of the elder parent. The result is like a defense used by a two-year-old child entering the "no-no" phase. Stubbornness. The elder parent must now learn to ask questions of the daughter, to give the daughter a chance of explanation.

Even more so, the caretaking person will avoid many difficulties in talking with the elder parent when (1) In the evening, the caretaking person reviews and prepares the elderly mother that "tomorrow shall we plan to do, to go, to get ready for..." And by asking-telling the elderly mother about the next day, she gives the mother a sense of security of knowing what may happen, of some predictability, and control of/for herself. (2) in the morning remind the mother of their planning in the evening before; This nullifies the sense of being ordered about. Gives the elderly mother some sense of what time of day, what they will do, even of what the elderly mother wants to do. And if the resistance remains, plan a breathing spell; give the mother a chance to think about it. (3) When the elderly mother still resists, do not push. Give her some time to think about it. (4) Share with the elderly mother about her own feelings. "How do you think

I feel when you are ...; don't want to do what we planned..." "I really feel sad, hurt, disappointed..."

One study of 189-paired an elderly parent with an adult daughter. The research used an open interview to explore the communication difficulties and strengths between the pair. The interviews revealed that 77 per cent of the daughters and 66 percent of the elderly identified stubbornness as a problem. The interactions described by daughters were appointments, attendance at social functions, clothing to wear, etc. claiming their mother rejected help or support with a defiant attitude. The mothers were adamant that not wanting to be controlled by their daughter was the reason.[3] "She always tells me what to do."

Another study asked the participants to keep a daily diary of communications for a week. Thirty-one per cent of adult daughters reported insistent, determined or even angry reactions from their elderly mother. The interactions focused on doctor appointments, attendance at other functions, clothing to wear, etc., which seem insignificant events. More heated were suggestions for mother to change her plan for the day. This was disturbing to the daughters - even though at times, the obstinate response by mother was due to physical limitations.

The diaries and interviews revealed that an obstinate or persistent response by the mother was a direct reflection of the negative and anxious mood of the adult daughter.[4] If the mother were aware of the anxiousness and fearfulness of the daughter, it may well change the mood of the interaction. Were the mother to become the parent again and hear the anxiousness of the child as before, the mother may respond differently, and allay the anxiety of the daughter.

On the other side, the daughter, although beset by caretaking responsibilities and other daily activities, could become more aware of the fear and anxiety of the elderly mother. For elderly persons need security and predictability to allay the indefiniteness of life of which they are ever aware. This mutual empathy demands much of both; it is a recurring problem of the developmental schism between generations that is ever anew.

When the responsibility of care is assumed by a daughter-in-law for her mother-in-law, additional difficulties for the caretaking daughter may arise from the competitiveness between mother and mother-in-law.

The difficulties between adult son-elderly parents are little discussed in research. What is obvious is that most difficulties arise between adult daughter-mother because mothers often outlive their mates. When a grandmother and a grandfather are both on the scene, they tend to have a moderating effect on each other's behavior, helping each other to see when they are crossing boundaries that shouldn't be breached.

Dissensions arise from the generational schism between the adults and elderly family members. In the Summing Up Period, the elderly have resolved many issues of their lives and have confronted a wish to have been more resilient or more authoritative in younger days. The adult children are confronting a host of stresses in their own lives and families. Whether faced with the view of themselves as aging, of children leaving home, of the new role of becoming grandparents, of unexpected economic issues, or of relationship issues within the home, their existential problems differ from their elderly parents. Supportive relationships between the generations reside in the ability to listen, be empathic and realistic in problem solving. As suggested in Chapter Three, even relationship difficulties can use three easy steps – What is the problem? What are the possibilities? Which is the optimal resolution?

Anna, age 74, has recently lost her husband, age 82. She is living alone in her three-bedroom house, on an acre of land that requires constant care. Did Mother Anna want to live with one of her seven children? No! Never! Of her children, only two resided nearby. Her daughter, Mary, age 54, is the second child of five in the family and has always been a caretaking person, and Edward, aged 49, also lived nearby but there were still teenage children living in his home. After a family discussion with Anna and the other children, Mary and her husband offered Mother Anna to live with them in a new smaller home they had just purchased. The one condition that would make it an optimal resolution was that Mother Anna would reimburse Mary and her husband for an additional room to be added to their home. The resolution provided Mother Anna with a sense of belonging, a place of her own. It provided Mary and her husband a sense of gaining economically and taking care of Mother. All seemed pleased with this resolution, so Mother Anna moved into the home of her second oldest daughter. It seemed an optimal and welcome resolution for the future of Mother.

Extreme situations do occur. More than once, I have

witnessed major changes being forced upon an elderly parent, without discussion, consent, or warning. One man, age 86, was living in his own home, cared for, and cooked for himself (Oh, perhaps frozen meals). He had a history of health problems – a heart valve replaced, some stomach problems, yet very affable and in good humor. One day, his two sons were taking him for a ride (he thought). Instead, they took him to an assisted living residence. The father was shown an apartment, was told by his sons that they had moved him to the apartment where he would have care, left him there alone, and abandoned to the care of the Director. His sons did tell him they would return in a week to see how he was adjusting. Shock, frustration, despair, distrust, set in for the elderly father.

Emotional factors reign important in relationships Strained family relationships interfere with parent-adult child relationships. What are the qualities of warmth and affection among the family members? How are they shown? Have there been rifts in the family due to divorces? Paternal grandparents often miss some closeness with grandchildren when the mother of the children may find it difficult to maintain an ongoing relationship with the father's parents. Has distance made contact increasingly difficult?

HOW WILL THE ROLE OF GRANDPARENT UNFOLD?

Relieved of the responsibility for the physical nurturance, the grandparents are often awed that grandchildren are their prodigy They are full of wonder, affection, and warmth toward the child. The new infant is embraced, held closely, and welcomed to the world of life. There are parents and grandparents to guide and care for the child as it experiences the wonders to come.

What will it be like to be a grandparent? What will the grandchild call the grandparent? An aside here: the child, itself, often finds a name for the grandparent. How often may the grandparents see the child? How possessive are the new parents? Can the infant become accustomed to grandparents' presence?

How long should a visit be? One hour, three hours, an afternoon or evening? How does the age of the child determine the visits? What do the parents wish for visits? Answers to the questions depend upon conversations with the parents, upon the personalities present, and especially upon the relationship among them.

One mother, whom I knew, would not let anyone, let alone the grandmother, hold the infant for the first three to six weeks after the infant's birth. Her reasoning? "I don't want her, the infant, to be confused about whom is her mother." Another new mother: "please take her, the infant, from me, I am afraid I might hurt her."

Regarding frequency of visits between grandchildren and grandparents, geographic distance is the strongest factor. In one study it was found that 74 per cent of grandparents had contact several times a week with grandchildren if they lived within fifteen minutes of the grandchild; 37 per cent had at least weekly contact if the distance between grandparents and grandchild were fifteen minutes to an hour away; and zero per cent if they lived more than an hour away. However, 86 percent of grandparents reported regular phone contact and 4 percent used the internet or email regularly. Undoubtedly, these percentages have increased significantly since the study was completed.[5]

STYLES OF GRANDPARENTING:

Grandparent roles are strongly influenced by the quality of family bonding with the nuclear family. Descriptions of the cohesion among generations include: First, the emotional closeness of the members -does warmth, affection, respect governing the interactions. What is the quality of agreements within the family concerning expectations of each other? Is there a freedom of communication so that there is an ability to talk out differences on important values and expectations? Can the bond of affection remain despite differences in values and behavior?

With emotional bonding as the strongest force among family members, what style will the grandparent use with the grandchildren?

1. The formal grandparent: This grandparent follows what is believed to be the appropriate guidelines for a grandparent. Often authoritative with expectations of respect, little direct interaction, nevertheless helpful to the parents and grandchild when needed.[6] The grandparent maintains an interest in the grandchild but does not become overly involved. In turn. There is emotional distance, as if the grandmother fears closeness. The grandchild child is cautious in

approaching the grandparent but delighted when receiving approval and affection.

2. The supportive grandparent. This is the proud, warming, cuddling, delighted grandparent. Proud of the parents and delighting with the grandchild. They have an active role, both playing and teaching as the grandchild grows. Often more lenient, warm, and affectionate with the grandchild, parents are filled with pleasure and a bit of envy of the grandparent-child relations. These giving grandparents are often helpful to the parents, and at times, intrusive into the child-rearing techniques of the parents. Even as the grandchild grows in years, and the interactions fit the age of the child, the relationship blossoms.

The emotional involvement of mother is an intricate part of this relationship. For example, one grandfather, delighted that his daughter gave birth to a grandson, would approach the parents, asking what he could present as a gift – to the one-year, two-year, four-year-old growing grandchild. The mother, greedy for all the love of her son, mother responded to her own father: he has everything, does not need anything. Thus she excluded the grandfather from bonding with the child. He was an outside visitor emotionally.

Another instance: Mother gave healthy birth to a baby girl. As the child grew, the mother become more and more protective of the child, rejecting of any grandparent affection toward the child, and almost greedily taking the child from a grandparent. Mother was jealous of the affection showered on the grandchild; fearful the child would be better loved than she.

Instances as these and many others cloud the relationships within the family. There comes a generational schism that is often acted out if succeeding generations, to the detriment of the openness of affection, trust, and support.

3. The surrogate parent. The number of grandparents who have the responsibility of rearing grandchildren has been increasing. It is estimated that over four million children are being reared by their grandparents who have the full responsibility for them – caretaking, nurturing, health, education, and most importantly, the growth of the emotional life of the child, the bonding with someone who loves, cares for them. About six million children younger than eighteen live in homes with grandparents who serve as the primary caretaker because of parents working to sustain economic viability. Many of these grandparents were younger than sixty years old; less than five percent were over 75 years old.[7] Obviously, very few elderly step into the role of surrogate parent completely and provide parttime services only.

In the surrogate role, the grandparent takes on major child rearing responsibilities. The initial shock of parenting of grandchildren is not as severe a problem to the grandparent as the ongoing, continuing daily demands of the parenting role. The grandparent suffers an excision of their own needs as well loss of social functioning and leisure expectation during a time of life when increased leisure was anticipated. It is important to note that some grandparents welcome the greater purpose for living, the rewards of love and gratitude, and the sense of being needed. Even so, the added stresses may critically affect the grandparent's health.[8]

The grandchild receives the confidence and emotional support from the grandparent as the grandparent substitutes for the parent. The grandchild's growth with the absence of the parent will shape the child's life.

4. Reservoir of family background and wisdom. True to the nature of grandparents during the Summing Up and Encore Period of life, the grandparent entertains the little one with many a story of their mommy and daddy when they were little children, and even of themselves when they were a child. Especially when adjusted to the age and interest of the little one, the child becomes fascinated by the stories – fascinated by the fact that older persons were once little and/or that older persons behaved similarly to themselves.

My father had been left in Sweden with a neighbor family when his parents with some of their children emigrated from Sweden. How often I regretted that I had not taken the quiet time to let him talk of those few years without his parents and living with relative strangers.

Another instance, as a substitute grandparent, I was delighted and surprised to have a nephew, now 75 years old, telephone me weekly just to talk. We could recall many instances of his grandparents, what they lived through in their lives (as WWII, holidays, etc.,} A special memory came when he spontaneously recalled that as a teenager, I had taught him tennis; a best thing that happened to him in those teenage years.

5. Distant grandparent: These grandparents often have only infrequent contact with the grandchildren, sometimes appearing primarily on holidays and special occasions. The relationship lacks the closeness of shared times, shared experiences, talking or playing. These grandparents are marginal to the family; only later will the grandchild long for more memories and or information about them. The third and fourth generation may become interested in their genealogical backgrounds; it is often too late to have the conversations of family history.

6. Dysfunctional Grandparents: It would be a wonder if all children were welcomed into the world with loving parents and grandparents. They may be harsh, rejecting, or punitive towards a child. It may be that an occasional child worms their way into their affection – rarely. Dysfunctional grandparents have themselves probably missed the warmth of love and life instead, burned by disfavor or unfortunate circumstances in their lives. Often their own family was not wanted; lives were shattered by trauma; or unfaithfulness ruined the days.

One grandparent recalled her dislike and fear of her own grandmother. If she or her sister took a cookie from the table or accidentally spilled their glass of milk, a strong, harsh wooden spoon hit them. Fear of displeasing grandmother ruled the relationship; yet pride when winning her praise, more than delighted them.

And now, there may come a time when a grandparent, whether supportive previously or not, cannot tolerate the presence of young grandchildren for a length of time. When the disability of ageing strikes, as hearing or visual problems, as confusion or pain sets in with the activity of the child – or television noise – quiet and peace is desired. This is not anger or dislike from the elderly, only the reaction to diminished abilities, easily aroused over stimulation, and the struggle of life itself.

GRANDFATHERS

New grandfathers report a sense of rejuvenation, pleasure, and excitement with the birth of a grandchild.[9] And many grandfathers feel awkward, even frightened, when holding an infant, lest they hurt or drop the baby. This soon passes as the infant develops and responds to the nurturing care offered by the grandfather. Grandmothers feel emotionally closer to grandchildren, partly through the role of mothering, while grandfathers have a more instrumental role with a grandchild. Grandfathers tend to highly value their role in passing down cultural traditions, providing instrumental support, and confirming masculine norms throughout the life of the grandchild.

Valued experiences of grandfather-grandson relationships reflect cherished memories. "I liked sitting on the bridge over the creek that grandfather had made and just being with him. Once when I first sat with him, and rose to go away, he asked me, "What is your hurry?" Here I learned that sometimes it is important just to be together in quietness."

"Grandfather helped me build the little wooden car for the race."

"I used to sit on the fender and watch him work on the automobile."

"Grandfather let me use his car on my first date."

When faced with the possibility of parenting a grandchild, grandfathers seem to experience a sense of powerlessness[10] in a transition to being a parent and ambivalent about their ability to continue parenting while the child is growing up. Often, the grandfather feels less optimistic about the role change to father, concerned about decreasing physical capabilities, fearful of not living long enough to help the grandchild. They have more stress with the responsibility, and are likely to be concerned about financial worries, poor health, social isolation from friends, and role changes and restrictions. It seems the grandfather also senses the change of freedom for himself that will bring about less opportunity to meet with friends, or to do planned activities following retirement.

Grandfathers add richness to the grandchildren's lives presenting the obvious difference in male and female roles in the home and society, cooperation in solving life's problems, a male-addition to activities, the explanation of values, and differing emotional connections.

SUMMARY COMMENTS

A family- mother, father, and child – are the sociocultural unit upon which life is centered. The lessons learned, values taught, emotional ties developed, are incorporated and guide life in adulthood. Family provides the central point for the being of a person. During the review of life in the Summing Up Period or a relaxation of life in the Encore Period, the family remains the focus, the bases – even when memories were distressful. Memories may be filled with joy, glee, pleasure, and everyday activities; or may be painful, sad, times when illnesses and disabilities, brought upon us through life, are endured with patience. As one grows older, the nearness of family becomes increasingly desired and comforting. The emotional pull toward family is there – even though not wanting to be a "burden" to the younger generation.

REFERENCES

1. Pop, Jime. 2018. "The Value of the Nuclear Family" in Christian Perspectives: Society and Life. Oct. 15, 2018.

2. About 10% of persons between 75-85 are presently living; this is expected to become about 20% of persons in 2050. Based on US Census 2010 data

3. https://pubmed.nchi.nim.nih.gov/25573152. "My parent is so Stubborn: - Perceptions of Aging Parents' Persistence, insistence, and Resistance.

4. https://pubmed.ncbi.him.nih.gov;30166932/ re Relationship Tensions ad Mood: Adult Children's Daily Experience of Aging Parents' Stubbornness."

5. Peter Uhlenberg, PhD, Bradley G. Hammill. "Frequency of Grandparent Contact with Grandchild Sets: Six Factors that Make a Differences." The Gerontologist, Vol. 38 Issue 3, June 1998, ages 276-285m https://doi.org/10,1093/geront/38.3.276
V. Susan Kraus Whitbourne, Ph.D. "Five type of grandparents and how they shape our lives?" www.psychologytoday.com/us/blog/fulfillment-any-age/201002/five-types-grandparenting

6. Susan Kraus Whitbourne, Ph.D. "Five type of grandparents and how they shape our lives?" www.psychologytoday.com/us/blog/fulfillment-any-age/201002/five-types-grand...

7. NIH Guide: GRANDPARENTING: ISSUES FOR AGING RESEARCH https://grants.nih.gov > grants > guide > pa-files > PA-95-086.html

8. Grandparents -IResearchNet. 1/11/2021 https://psychology.iresearchnet.com/developmental-psychology/family-psychology/grndparents/

9. Jensen, Bethany K.; Quaal, Gillian; and Manooglan, Margaret. (2018) "Understanding the Grandfather Role in Families," PURE insights: Vol 7, Article 4.

10. Bullock, Karen (2005) "Grandfathers and The Impact of Raising Grandchildren," The Journal of Sociology & Social Welfare. Vol.32.Iss. I, Article 5.

Chapter Eleven

The Shades Of Life Are Drawn

The current, the energy that move the water slows...moving back and forth using the last movements...slower yet, and then quietness, no more current, no more stones or hills to roll over... this is all....

And so, the fragile shades of life gradually are pulled down...Delicately coloring our once zeal for movement, for life... somehow, we know the end is nearer, the fragile, colorful, messages are clear...life is diminishing, is ebbing away. We can only wait.

As the end of life nears, the pain of being older is added to the physical pains within us. The physical system is shutting down. Albert Schweitzer once said, "Pain is a more terrible load for mankind than even death itself and awakens us to a courage and faith unrealized before..." Pain becomes quieted – with the help of medicine and with the help of the body itself. The strength we have in accepting vulnerabilities has helped to find an ability to live gladly within our limitations. As the shades of death near, often the spirit is quieted, the suffering, calmed.

This chapter is highly personal for at the age of ninety-three years, I, too, have known dying and death of family and friends – too many to bring to memory at this point. I well remember my husband, one exceedingly early morning. He awakened me, saying, "I am dying." He did – in my arms. How sweet the moment. How quieted he was. Yes, his death was anticipated, but not that morning. The breath of life escapes One cannot keep it.

Beautiful poems have been written by the living about death. I think of John Keats poem, "A thing of beauty is a joy forever...it will never pass into nothingness..." Dylan Thomas' poem, "Do not go gentle into that good night..." Emily Dickinson, "Because I could not stop for Death, He kindly stopped for me..." And I wonder, how shall I die? Shall it be quietly, knowing the comfort of death or shall I rage at the misfortunates of dying? So much has been said; so much un-sayable. The experience of dying is our own, alone. We know it only when it happens, if knowing it even then is possible.

The end of life comes in many ways. Death may come suddenly or traumatically, or gradually with the fading of a fatal illness, with prolonged pain as a precursor to death, with a slow decrease in functional abilities, or more quickly with a cascade of illnesses. It may come suddenly, as it did with my father who died of a heart attack while planting a cherry tree for his daughter-in-law. Or it may come traumatically, as in falling. Falling is the fifth leading cause of death in older adults, and the risk of falling is doubled for the older persons taking psychotropic medicines.[1]

Death lies near In a Hospice setting. Patients are severely ill, little or no anticipation of recovering health. Look around. Many are sitting quietly, eyes open, not really seeing; sounds and noises around them, there is no reaction; nurses or others walking nearby – their eyes may not follow their path; time passes, without awareness; little movement of their hands or body; and occasionally sleeps falls upon the person, head droops; soon enough, wakefulness may return. These persons seem near death. Sensations are dulled – vision and hearing present without much reaction, no need to be fulfilled, little movement. Just there. If someone is with them, they slowly respond.

A strong, common fear is that of dying alone, with no family or friend present. Not that the person could do much – only be present, provide a warm touch, radiate the warmth of love. More dreaded is the possibility of dying in an institution, as a hospice or hospital, in isolation from all signs of life, itself, or with pain and distress unallayed. The process of dying that brings a final loss to dignity when the person is not able to manage the basic physical matters, as in incontinence. When this happens, the dying person may have no awareness of his/her condition. The shame or fear of death occurring in such a manner resides in the person who is yet alive and overwhelmed at the thought of that happening to them. My wonderful mother, reticent and shy much of her life, was horrified when her aged friend and neighbor was found dead, naked, on her way to the bathroom. The possible shame were that to occur to her was an overwhelming thought for her, an horror. Thankfully, Mother died in a hospice, with several of her children at her bedside.

Losing the quality of life due to Alzheimer's disease or another dementia also brings dread. We do not know death itself, how then not to know dying? How to die, when unaware of the self, of others you love? Perhaps there are redeeming qualities to this death?

One reaction by those who are dying, is a denial. "I am not that sick; I'll get over this..." Life seems to be an incomplete status – not ready to go —-something yet to do...Denial may give a temporary impetus for health to improve, to live better, to exercise more...This denial may bring a spurt of energy, even health, that may work for a short time??

And another reaction is angering that one is dying. There is a tendency to rale against the fortunes of life, to blame someone." It is the doctor's fault...too much wrong medicine..." The anger arises from a sense of helplessness. It represents a loss of control. Some try to bargain with themselves with the doctors, or with God. "If only"...a promise to mend their ways, to treat someone better, or "Just let me live long enough to...." Yes, some do die with anger, even after a prolonged illness.

Acceptance that one is dying often brings some relief and peace. No longer must the person struggle for health, to please another, or even to stay awake. A calmness may quiet any distress. It is time to say goodbye to loved ones and to life. It is time to cross that river.

A final task for those who are dying, is to gain a sense of

completion in life. It is to acknowledge that we are dying, to accept death so that we can talk honestly, without fear, about death with our loved ones, especially. It also means to listen to them. What do they want or need from the dying person? The messages will be healing for the dying person as well as others.

One important task is to ask forgiveness for a wrong you may have done – or been party to the wrong – that may have been damaging or hurtful to another. I remember one incident with my mother who was nearing death. It was a memory of feeling so alone. I was two or three years of age, standing by her as she breastfeed my younger sister. Alone. I shared this memory with my mother. Wonderfully, she replied, "I never had enough arms to hug you all." She had seven children. What a smiling, happy moment for us both.

Just as important is a message of "I forgive you." I forgive you for...whatever the supposed damage. This message, "forgive you" will relieve you from leaving behind any bitterness and grant the other peacefulness in memories of you. It opens the gateway for love.

"Thank you" for all the life you have share with me..."For being my daughter, for loving me, for caring about me, for bringing me so much joy." What a great gift to leave for others. And then, "I love you" can never be said enough.

Finally, "Goodbye." Yes, comfort comes in saying goodbye, openly and directly. It provides family and friends and others the freedom to accept your death and to continue with or life. "Goodbye, I love you." It is also important to be given the freedom to die when the time is there. One mother of three daughters lay ill, in much pain as the medication would weaken. The three daughters, wanting to be with her, would all three be there, touching her, talking to her for hours at a time. Mother was in a coma, could not respond. One day, the visiting nurse suggested that mother needed permission to die from her three daughters. The daughters each said, cried, "goodbye" to her and left mother alone in her room. Within a couple hours, the mother died – in effect the daughters granted permission for her to leave.

The Elderly Ages are the time of great life challenges and of great stress at a period of life when the elderly person has fewer graces for response. Every day is more important, more meaningful, and more reason to give joy and happiness.

the fragile shades of life gradually are pulled down...Delicately coloring our once zeal for movement, for life... somehow, we know the end is nearer, the fragile, colorful, messages are clear... life is diminishing, is ebbing away. We can only wait.

REFERENCES

1. Bates, Margaret, M. (1966) The Many Faces of Dependency in Old Age. Cambridge University: Cambridge University Press.

CHAPTER TWELVE

The Stopping Point

*The waters lie still. All currents that once roiled
its flow are not quieted. Movements to come are
unknown, perhaps unknowable. We shall see.*

The simple poem that follows is an attempt to consolidate
chapters. To bring them together, to share that being elderly
is full of grace, of richness of life, of gratitude toward life.

A POEM OF LIFE

Let us think of whom we are, from
childhood to this time.
We now see the path we've come, remember act and line.
For Summing Up may help our kids take the brush away,
So they can sing a song of joy as they trod their way.

From mother's depth to father's arms,
never losing that first home.
Crawling, walking, or roller skates,
home was e'er our dome
From home and school to places far,
home stayed with us for e'er.
Age and time took much away, memory fills the hour.

Our childhood acts molded firm our personality
For molded though our traits may
be, we were conscientiously,
Beholden to each task we were, effort to sustain
With hearty steps to endure, for the goal to gain.

On the path we have stumbled with choices to regret,
Learned too late that impulse crumbles, .
learned some to reject.
Harshness and anger did unfold along the path we trod,
All now forgiven so that we inner peace may hold.

Our bodies fine we controlled in tennis, golf and playing
Now reluctantly submit, the body is controlling.
Hearing aids, canes and spectacles
guide the path each day
If fortunate each day is ours, with no pain to pay.

Though we suffer some in illness, cheerful is the time
We spend each hour with sun and
clouds, lakes and rivers, fine.

Flowers and trees, birds and bees enrich all sensations
Bringing clarity for an evening's meditation.

Loving and giving enhance content, revelry for life
Deeply committing to one's bourn,
may induce more strife
Strife brings an openness to life and
ever more brings grace
To share with those whose life is
strife, joy and peace embrace.

With partner, children and friends, life passes ever more.
Our children hold our lives within,
strength their inner core
Grandparents we are, signs of life's creativity,
And a smile at the fate of time's incongruity.

Encore, our last days to be spent with life's end ever near.
Problem solving easier -select, compensate, cheer.
And Summing Up our days that we were living here
We bestow to our children love and hope for they are dear

Our final home, not far away from those we love dear.
The day's unknown, yet welcome,
there's nothing left to fear
Aloneness comes as we get near that last day to appear
All love is cast within you, never to disappear.

A fragile shade has led our way throughout life's passages,
Delicate and hovering near, yielding messages.

In subtleness and colorfully sow the lighted time
That leads us tenderly to this end of life – sublime.

Viola Mecke
July 18, 2021

INDEX

Made in the USA
Monee, IL
27 March 2022

93650972R00111